Wisdom

of the

Vernal Woods

SHIRES ♦ PRESS

4869 Main Street
P.O. Box 2200
Manchester Center, VT 05255
www.northshire.com

Wisdom of the Vernal Woods

Copyright © 2017 by J. E. Diaz
All rights reserved

ISBN Number: 978-1-60571-385-4

Building Community, One Book at a Time
A family-owned, independent bookstore in
Manchester Ctr., VT, since 1976 and Saratoga Springs, NY since 2013.
We are committed to excellence in bookselling.
The Northshire Bookstore's mission is to serve as a resource for
information, ideas, and entertainment while honoring the needs of
customers, staff, and community.

Printed in the United States of America

Wisdom of the Vernal Woods

J. E. Diaz

For Suzie

Source of Inspiration
Trusted Sounding Board
Venerable Grounding Rod

Thank You.
Again.

To family, friends and readers who took the time to comment on *Wandering Spring, Notes from the Woods of Winhall, Vermont*. Your suggestions and support mean more than you realize.

Thank You All.

. . .

A special thank you to Debbi Wraga of Shires Press.

Her time, talent, effort and patience have been invaluable to both projects.

Preface

After publishing *Wandering Spring, Notes from the Woods of Winhall, Vermont,* Grandma Ida would question my penning of another book about the woods. Referring to her expectation that I should write to become rich and famous, I imagine her gesturing with thumb, index, and middle finger held tight at their tips, hinged wrist flopping toward and away from her face, yelling with that oft missed, searing accented voice, "Ay-ah! And when?" With scowled brow and piercing eyes negating any possible reply I could muster, "Wisdom?" she'd continue, "You want wisdom? Get a job!" Of course, Grandma Ida yelled, "Get a job," at everyone, even if they *were* employed. It was her favorite English phrase and she practiced every day, yelling it at TV news broadcasts.

Well, my answer to her would be the same as it is to anyone... Labors of love have a way of making ends meet. And this one continues to leave me richer for doing it. Knowing Grandma Ida, she'd quickly soften and say, "Go, do what you love."

So here we are again.

Contents

Introduction

Invitation:	1
Nothing Stirs:	3
Before the Divine:	5
In the Presence of an Old Soul:	9
Under the Cover of a Sheltering Balsam:	13
Just a Ruse:	21
Clouds Race By:	25
Dust Covered Thoughts:	31
In the Woods to My Left:	37
Urged from My Pondering State:	41
Watching Ice Melt:	45
Where Wood Frogs Gather:	49
A Quieter Spring than Usual:	52
Pinhole Points of Light:	55
Goblins and Doom:	59
Enduring Examples:	63
An Interesting Game:	67
Indifferent Magnificence:	73
A Moment of Privilege Afforded by Circumstance:	77
An Embarrassing Moment:	82
In Exchange for a Bit of Obliviousness:	85
In the Dense Balsam Fir Thicket:	91
A Diplomatic Approach:	101
What Fish Think:	106

19 Days of Merriment:	*108*
By What Standard?:	*111*
A Lot of Bluster:	*117*
Getting Lost:	*123*
The Carcass:	*125*
A Bird's Eye View:	*131*
In the Beauty of Growing Darkness:	*141*
Wisdom of the Vernal Woods:	*146*
contact:	*151*

Introduction

I read a story as a young lad about a certain devout person of one faith visiting an enlightened observer of another faith, both considered to be wise. This certain devout person sat for tea and watched as the host filled their cup to overflow. The host continued pouring until the visitor exclaimed, "What are you doing?" to which the host replied, "You are like this cup. You come to me full, with no room for anything else."

I didn't set out to write a book titled, *Wisdom of the Vernal Woods*. My plan was to write a second *Wandering Spring* with a similar subtitle as the first. But in my notes and drafts there appeared something unexpected and I realized that despite my good intentions I was approaching this endeavor much the same as our devout person in the story above approached their visit with the enlightened observer. To be succinct, my cup was full before the spring wanderings ever began.

Though popular culture tends to present both seekers and possessors of wisdom in a certain light, the truth is there's no mold from which either is cast. And there's no special place from which wisdom emanates. Whether you're on a lonely mountaintop or in a crowded city, wisdom is there. Whether your collar is blue or white, have means or have little, devout, enlightened, educated, uneducated… wisdom awaits. It doesn't belong to one people, one culture, one religion. It's endless in form and function; it has no price yet is priceless and best of all, lies in wait for the taking; hidden in plain sight. Where we find it is far less important than what we do with it. I happen to find wisdom in the woods because for some reason, that's where I seem to relate best to its concepts. But to suggest that a forest is the only place to find it would be insulting to countless people who gather around the luminance of wisdom from different perspectives of experience.

Any given day provides opportunity for uncovering a bit of wisdom. But wisdom doesn't always accommodate. I don't want to bamboozle the reader into thinking that every day in the forest yields a lesson of some kind. That's not real. And you shouldn't enter the forest in hope of finding the holy grail of higher consciousness. It's not there. At least I haven't seen it in my wanderings or heard of its existence from any of our woodland kin. But I have on occasion found precious nuggets of knowledge to be collected and placed with care into the vault of wisdom. Maybe you'll find a few within these pages.

. . .

The events and subsequent stories, poems, and reflections in *Wisdom of the Vernal Woods,* occurred in chronological order during the spring of 2017. As a collection they reflect the mood changes and sometimes harsh realities of springtime in the forested mountains. But there's whimsy in the wood, and perplexity as well, so be prepared. While most have a particular focal point or two, some take a more thematic approach. And perhaps you'll notice something of import to you within a story, poem, or reflection that I didn't see. Wisdom is, after all, a collection of perspectives.

Concerning the location of these wanderings other than to say they all transpired within the state of Vermont, allow me to offer this: Where we are is a result of where we've been and is oftentimes where we end up while where we're going is more looked upon as when we'll get there and what we'll have when we arrive than what we'll experience along the way... taking us back to where we are.

Now, let's go wandering. But be warned. There is wisdom lurking in the woods that may challenge preconception so mind the fullness of your cup and keep your mind open.

"Silence is the balance of all things; stoic in the face of tempest, self-possessed in times of trial. It is the beginning of wisdom, the step before reason; the willingness to learn."

Nothing Stirs

Crust of night-hardened snow breaks beneath me as I wander the dormant, moonlit forest. Jupiter leads the celestial procession ever west and away from last winter night, while last quarter Moon in the south, Polaris in the north, and Vega high in the east guide me.

The air is crisp, calm, cold. Nothing stirs, not even winter-washed beech leaves on chest-high saplings clinging to last year's dreams. Stars of the Milky Way span the breadth of heaven as fractal limbs of dormant wood commune with the Great Galactic Fractal.

A Barred owl floats in silence across the jeweled sky, perching above me. I feel exposed as it looks down; staring, motionless. My thoughts wander to the openness behind it; the unending, ever-expanding universe. Space was aptly named. The owl blinks, still staring, my thoughts, still wandering.

The most abundant element in the Universe isn't hydrogen or any matter, dark or otherwise, but silence; the decorum state before the chaotic big bang.

Silence is the balance of all things; stoic in the face of tempest, self-possessed in times of trial. It is the beginning of wisdom, the step before reason; the willingness to learn.

The owl blinks again. Turning its gaze toward Polaris, it flies north in silence, disappearing into the night.

"The simple emotion of gratitude transcends our conscious thought and gives humility to reason. Gratitude is the most elemental form of worship. It needs no adulterating. It has no equal. Gratitude is the purest act of genuflection."

Before The Divine

East beyond a gentle down slope, dawn will emerge through columns of beech and maple. To the north, the woods are thick; a blend of mid age and young. Moon shadows from the uneven forest edge reach out along the open snow to greet me from the south. And everywhere, shadow creatures move about the forest.

. . .

Twilight begins as silence and stillness break; creak and sway of rooted timber and the whisk of branches whipping wind announce the first pixel of dawn. Fading moon and refracting light of sun darken the white snowfield. Vestige stems of spent brambles grow out of tree shadows on the snow.

. . .

Dawn lightens with a gust of shifting wind; ground snow whisks from west to east while treetops sway north and south. Pale blue rules as Jupiter pulls the night sky west above a coal-orange horizon glowing through black shadowed columns of beech and maple. Faint moon shadows evaporate under the bluing cosmic dome.

. . .

Daylight broadens pale-ginger in the east, while snow remains white between dark columns. Above, sky bleeds out blue to the snow below in the clearing south and west. At the far edge, scattered white birch trees glow turquoise. The Dipper fades as does Polaris, now a memory at the tip of a beech branch. Mottled grays and browns and the textural details of bark and snowcover reveal themselves. Jupiter, fading, divides the line between day light and earth shadow cast into space.

. . .

Last winter night has given way
to last winter morning's light of day,
though spring will own the Sun today,
as Equinox arrives at six twenty-nine,
twenty-five minutes before the Divine.

. . .

With gratitude for the warmth of its presence on this cold, clear morning, I greet the Divine Sun at six fifty-four and ponder how this simple emotion transcends our conscious thought and gives humility to reason. Gratitude is the most elemental form of worship. It needs no adulterating. It has no equal. Gratitude is the purest act of genuflection.

"The Universe has many voices. All are worthy of speaking, all worthy of listening, and all may be understood... but not by all."

In the Presence of an Old Soul

There are times when thick, valley dwelling clouds smother the landscape leaving only the highest peaks visible; boreal islands in the sky, floating in an endless sea of downy white billows.

. . .

As I wander out of valley cloud onto one of these majestic islands, I'm treated to cold crisp air, cerulean sky, and deep, firm snowpack that supports my weight on snowshoes and allows for easy climbing. The scent of Balsam fir; rich citrus evergreen, wafts from sun heated branches, weaving its tempting aroma through tangles of Beard lichen.

Light wind whispers through the forest. Cold crystal mist chills my face and neck as snow spills off trees and continues on in a translucent wall of white. Mesmerized by the sight of frozen wisps of wind, I nonetheless become aware of a growing quiet that ends in deep silence. I feel the presence of an old soul.

Shadowed among treetops, hugging the ridgeline from west to east, it disappears through the forest on whooping wings; tell tale clue that a raven is near. Still and steady I wait and listen till cold and stiff in the shaded summit chill. Turning my head without forethought of reason, a raven comes into view perched several meters away and a few above. It looks at me with a sideways glance quite common among ravens. Out of respect for this old soul and its ability to have gotten so close without me knowing, I allow it time to decide what to do with me now that it has my undivided attention.

With a pre-note knock as though clearing its throat the raven issues soft phrases common for an adult with young while its body language stays relaxed and inviting, emphasizing the importance of what's being said. After a few moments of what sounds to me like repeated phrases, it grows silent again. Still reluctant to speak, I tilt my head, eyebrows pinched together in a questioning facial expression. The raven looks back in similar manner then leaps into the air on whooping wing beats, lifting itself through the canopy. I lose sight of it below ridgeline as a final resounding "GWONK!" echoes through the basin below; an exclamation point placed on what was spoken. But what did it say?

As I wander about the mountain, I ponder the incident with Raven... The Universe has many voices. All are worthy of speaking, all worthy of listening, and all may be understood... but not by all.

"The Universe began with a great light, and with light comes shadow."

"Things are not always what they seem."

Under the Cover of a Sheltering Balsam

The first new moon after vernal equinox brought with it an ice event for about 24 hours… or was it longer?

. . .

Billows of frozen fog seep through the canopy. Unfurling tendrils of freezing mists weave through weeping trees. Frosted tentacles of ice-crusted understory thicken as moist air hardens in an invisible process.

A branch breaks above. Cascades of ice bounce off me. I'm spared by the Unknown as a spear of wood and ice lancing the skin of snow imbeds into the ground before me.

Small trees move with muffled moans, kept quiet by an encasement of ice. Large trees sway with a curious creak; the sound of leather clad giants reaching and twisting. One takes a step, or so it sounds, as a limb breaks in the distance hurtling splintered wood and shattered crystal to the forest floor in a symphony of white noise.

Fresh fox tracks appear as I wander in the direction of a distant swamp. A Hairy woodpecker chips away at the self sealing hole of ice it's made to get at whatever this moment's meal happens to be. A porcupine moves ever so slightly in a tree fork nearby, catching my attention. Beige-white curls of frozen birch bark stick out their icicle tongues daring me to make fire with them. I chuckle, returning the insult.

. . .

From a nearby hill I survey the swamp through binoculars. Though fog and mist lay heavy in the air, the ceiling is high enough to see all around. But it's the sound I notice first...

At a recently felled food source; a large yellow birch several meters from the pond, one beaver gnaws and collects twigs for the family pantry, while another; still in the water, removes a chunk of ice from the channel used to access the harvest. The tree has few branches left, forming a skeletal umbrella over the center of the log. Shards of bark litter the ground below.

Within minutes, both beavers submerge beneath the ice, relaxed and focused on the business of living. Not wanting to overindulge my good fortune of watching undetected, I wander off, happy to have seen them.

. . .

Far from the swamp, a side hill clearing seems an easy shortcut. Angling upslope into the now dropping ceiling I find myself in an impenetrable, mist-shrouded matrix of frozen brambles; icy spikes reinforced with piercing thorns beneath a fragile clear coating. Shortcut indeed... I retreat to the bottom of the hill.

Crawling under the cover of a sheltering balsam while looking back uphill, silhouettes of distant trees become undefined shadows in the mist; ominous, threatening, yet never advancing. At peace in the bosom of the balsam, I close my eyes and breathe deep the sweet, moist air.

. . .

A thunderous roar disturbs my sleep. Lumbering giants dressed in leather appear through mist on the hill. Earth shakes as they move forward; a klangfarbenmelodie of creaking garments, crashing footsteps, and the rumbling echoes of quaking ground. They stop at the bottom of the hill and raise their heads, sniffing the air. A deep silence flows over the forest as though it was following them, trying to catch up. They look suspicious to me; guilty of something, thievery perhaps. I crawl out from my resting place and confront them.

"You there," I call out to the one in front. "What have you in your satchel?"

"None of your business," it replies in a booming voice while squinting and sniffing, looking in my direction but never at me.

I can't tell if they're females or males. They look similar; not masculine but not feminine either, just giant.

"Get out of our way or we'll run you over," it warns, still sniffing and looking as though trying to find me.

It occurs to me they don't see well. I put my theory to the test.

"Who are you to threaten me?" I reply in a confident tone, inconsistent with my comparative size.

Anger grows on all their faces as a wave of mist wafts down the hill, freezing them in an instant.

"You have been spared by the Unknown," a soft feminine voice speaks out of the mist, each syllable coming from a slightly different direction than the one before. "You are right about these giants. They have stolen… shadow creatures," the voice continues.

"How do you steal shadow creatures?" I ask.

"More distressing than how is why," the voice replies.

"Who are you?" I ask, looking all around but seeing no one.

"I am New Moon. My spell on these giants will last as long as it takes to find the answer. The forest cannot stay this way for long. Ice will continue to form on everything while the spell holds, but it is the only way to keep the giants contained. You must hurry."

"Wait… Hurry? Me? Hurry for what? Shouldn't we let the shadow creatures out of that satchel?" I ask, stalling for time. "Maybe they can help solve this. After all, they may have seen or heard something."

"You are not afraid?"

"No. I'm at peace with shadow creatures," I reply, with the expectation that we'll release them and find out why they were taken.

"No matter, it cannot be done," snaps New Moon in a dismissive tone. "The spell keeps the satchel closed. We do not know what else may be in there."

"I don't believe in spells and magic, I believe in the observable Universe that sustains us."

"Then realize the Universe began with a great light, and with light comes shadow. Whatever can steal shadow has attained too great a power to be ignored. You must go and find out the truth."

"So..." I ease into my next question, "If these giants can be stopped with an icy mist, I'm assuming they're not the ones with the power to steal shadow."

"Correct. They are couriers. You must find the Stealer of Shadow."

"Look, I came out here to wander the woods and gather material for writing a book about being here," I blurt with a touch of vehemence, "not chase after the Stealer of Shadow."

"Then write about it, all of it," replies New Moon with equal fervor. "But in the mean time, the forest is icing over and you must help."

. . .

Walking back the way I came, an odd feeling of hope that I'll see the beavers again pervades my thinking.

. . .

At the downed birch where I saw them earlier, the beavers seem unwary as I approach within feet of them before stopping. They look at me with expectation, as though they've been waiting for me to arrive. As foolish as it seems, I begin my inquiry as they busy themselves chewing and gnawing.

"Do either of you know who would have stolen shadow creatures and given them to leather clad giants who don't see well and sniff the air when spoken to?" I ask.

Of course they say nothing but continue snacking and gnawing on thin-skinned twigs and thick-barked trunk. Watching them, I feel as though I've known these particular creatures for a long time. We're friends, or so it feels, and we understand one another. Their confident demeanor conveys a sense of peace. My mind wanders. Taxonomically, they're rodents. Out here they're so much more... Things are not always what they seem.

My line of reasoning snaps as I realize the beavers have stopped all activity except for staring at me.

Quite without thinking I ask, "What? New Moon isn't what she seems?"

Surprised at my words and even more so at the look of satisfaction on the beaver's faces as they waddle to water's edge and slip into their world under the ice, I stand dumbfounded at how certain I now feel that I must be dreaming.

As my eyes open, I begin to shake off the fog of a weird dream and realize in this world, I don't need to know who stole the shadow creatures because no one stole them. Though I'm nagged by thoughts of light and shadow and things that may not be what they seem.

But it was a dream. It doesn't matter.

...As I wander home, ice thickens on trees and the sound of distant breaking limbs becomes more prevalent.

"Shadow is a reflection of fear, and a way for us to reconcile those fears."

Just a Ruse

Sometime during the night I woke to the crashing of limbs and the power going out. Ice was accreting quickly and damage to the forest was accelerating. Against all reason, I decided to listen to New Moon, get out of bed, and go looking for who may have stolen the shadow creatures.

. . .

Navigating the nighttime woods is difficult enough when conditions are good, but tonight it seems a foolhardy endeavor. Thick, frigid mist rejects the beam of my headlamp, throwing it back at my eyes. Water drips out of the darkness, some in pitter patter droplets, more in virtual downpours soaking my clothes, and the ice... crashing; splintering and downing trees. I stumble over fallen limbs and every other big and little obstruction the forest floor has to offer. This is stupid. I've had enough.

"New Moon," I call out, when reaching the last place we spoke. "I've given thought to who may have stolen the shadow creatures. The truth is; no one has. There's no Stealer of Shadow. I didn't catch it at first but later remembered what you said about the Universe beginning with a great light and where there is light there is shadow."

"Yes, I remember," replies the familiar feminine voice, each syllable coming from a slightly different direction than the one before it. "Continue."

"If there is shadow when there is light then conversely there is no shadow when there is no light. Therefore during a new moon the shadow creatures aren't visible… but they're still there. The idea of your spell keeping the satchel closed and asking me if I was afraid of shadow creatures was just a ruse."

While I speak, the forest sheds its icy encasement as warm air breaks the bonds of frozen water.

"There were no shadow creatures in the satchel," I continue, "because they exist in our minds. Shadow is a reflection of fear, and a way for us to reconcile those fears."

"You are correct," replies New moon.

"But what of the gian…"

Before I can finish the question, a great crashing; an explosion of trunk, limb, stick and twig bursts from the darkness with such force it shakes me off my feet.

. . .

Heart pounding, I spring up in bed and sit frozen in the dark. Wait, this isn't my bed… I'm wet, cold. The balsam, I'm still under the balsam…

My senses begin to focus on the sound and feel of a steady rain, a warming wind. There's no creaking of ice encrusted trees, no branches breaking, no limbs plummeting to the ground in crashing cacophony.

The giants, New Moon, the familiar beavers; it was a dream, all of it. How long was I asleep?

"Speech has the power to chide or instruct, injure or heal, raze or restore hope. It is our best tool and worst weapon, finest trumpet of all things good, warning horn of a darkened heart. All good and bad begin and end with a timely spoken word of men."

Clouds Race By

Two days after the first 1st quarter moon of spring, there's a break in the cold wet weather that's persisted for three days and is forecast to begin again in a few hours and continue for another three days. But for now, I grab some essentials and head for the forest.

. . .

With high top boots, proper winter clothing, wide brim hat, and fresh lit Savinelli Roma securely clenched between my teeth, I wander up a wooded knoll, slogging along in lingering snowpack. I'm beginning to question the sanity of leaving snowshoes behind.

Fresh bear tracks dissolve my self-pity. Considering the fact it's been snowing and/or raining for most of the day these are "warm" tracks. I look in the direction the bear is headed first, and then examine the prints. Unmistakable from the variation in size between front and back paw, with a slight inward pointing gait, and of course claw marks, this bear's stride looks relaxed. In consideration that it may be enjoying the break in weather as much as I am, I decide not to follow and focus on things around me.

Hobblebush flower buds with their yet-to-unfurl primary leaves free of snow and ice resemble tiny grey-brown fat-bodied bats with wings stuck in upright vertical position, or the heads of such bats with elongated ears.

Last year's seed heads of white spiraea bent on woody stems face upslope away from prevailing winds; delicate puffs of conical spearhead that crumble between my fingers.

Beech leave sheathes, sharp as nearby bramble thorns though not as durable, wait to open. The two together remind me of stern words spoken. One sharp enough to capture attention; a timely guiding admonition, the other cutting, spewed in anger; a spirit piercing censure. My thoughts wander toward the peculiar habit among our species of using words.

Speech has the power to chide or instruct, injure or heal, raze or restore hope. It is our best tool and worst weapon, finest trumpet of all things good, warning horn of a darkened heart. All good and bad begin and end with a timely spoken word of men.

Billowing white puffs atop granite-grey slabs spin translucent blue threads into the cerulean sky as clouds race by on a cushion of air squeezed between their weight and the unyielding ground.

Horizontal moss on fallen logs and exposed rock lie hidden beneath the spring snowpack. Those who chose a vertical existence on the sides of trees glow bright green with lengthening daylight and recent abundant moisture. Tree-dwelling lichens brighten to blue-green as algae in the organism creates food for itself and its companion fungus while their snow covered comrades below remain cold, pale, unnourished.

The dormant woods roar atop the knoll as fierce, gusting winds slam the west face, ricocheting over its summit. Cloud-blocked frigid air warms to chill when the sun appears. Immersed in the beauty of this moment in time, I wander toward the lee side.

Sun warmed clothing holds its heat without the whisking wind in this different world several meters below the summit. A lone Tufted titmouse calls. A small grove of beech saplings thick with last year's faded leaves shiver in unison with the slightest breeze. Test holes of a Pileated woodpecker riddle an old maple while a full commitment to excavation appears in a taller, more suitable tree nearby. Scattered oases of clustered young Red spruce create a snowshoe hare's dream in an otherwise birch, beech, and maple dominated wood.

Nibbling on the tip of a Yellow birch twig; aromatic wintergreen toothpick, compliments of the management, I notice a wet, black stain coming from an apparent hole in a large beech. The misfortune of age befalls me once again as I remember not to touch it the moment my fingers engage the wicked liquid. It has the piquant bouquet of *Canis poopus udus* which I have trouble rubbing off my fingers despite an endless supply of snow for the job. If I remember right, this poo-heady brew is an early sign of nectria; a fungal infection that follows an infestation of beech scale which, my understanding is, damages the bark sufficiently for the nectria to invade. What I forgot was the smell.

After scouring my hands with spruce needle juice I sit and enjoy the late afternoon sun, un-cooled by howling winds thrown over the knoll.

A gaggle of crows heading south, quartering into the relentless west gale above me, take time and make effort to betray my presence. "Look everyone... A hominid is near," I imagine them saying in their cawing and crowing. A woods robin nears, peeping in objection to me, being uninvited as I am.

Blue windows close behind puff shutters of white and grey, blocking the sun, cooling the now shifting winds. The temperature is dropping.

Leaving the knoll by another route, I happen upon a trickling spring flow; a narrow, snow free lane through the forest. What at first appears a leaf flitting about in the wind turns out to be a Winter wren darting silent and swift under and over moss covered limbs of fallen trees as it crisscrosses the open seep, hunting for insects.

Further along, a brown bristly caterpillar seems quite at home on snow and stops to greet me. It reacts to the heat of my hand as I move it from one side to the other, then above and behind. It doesn't follow the movement, but turns after a few moments of my hand being in one place. Curious a thing as it is, I bid the caterpillar good day and wish it luck in whatever endeavor bristly brown caterpillars endeavor to do.

Wet snow falls in a fizzling symphony as whiteout conditions halt my progress. Submerged in a snowglobe, I rekindle my pipe beneath wide brimmed hat and wait for visibility to improve.

"Nature is neither malevolent nor benevolent, it is indifferent. It is often our perception of it and reaction to it that determines our fate."

Dust Covered Thoughts

The trail of ice and muddy snow is a dangerous place for bipedal creatures, challenging balance and threatening a slip into slurry. Choosing the ice, I place my feet with care on fallen twigs, shards of bark, and last year's leaves either embedded in or scattered about the surface. Sun warmed rocks protrude through the ice, increasing traction, though today at this moment there's not sun enough to warm them. A shower of pellet snow spreads its opaque, dreary sibilance throughout the forest as its front wall arrives...

. . .

...Individual trees reappear, slipping through the shower's back wall as it moves away. An empty hush descends upon the wood. Bright grey skies replace the dull white veil of snow now in the distance.

Further along, a trickle of tiny rivulet and whisper of distant gushing seasonal streams break the silence. To me, every running rivulet is a thing of beauty, every flowing stream a reason for joy.

Wandering deeper into the dormant wood, no waterways occupy my auditory senses. I listen to wind as it courses the canopy. A tree squeaks in the sway. No birds are singing. It's a lonely feeling... a warm, welcoming, lonely feeling. After a brief pause to examine two sets of bear tracks in the mud, I travel down slope toward the sound of water once again. It's a singular source, strong and full.

Arriving at the flow where it runs through a drained and dried beaver pond; now a grassy wet field with large rocks exposed, I stop to ponder the former event. Was it abandonment or disaster, or both? At the far downstream edge, a berm covered with weeds, brambles, grasses, and saplings define the wall that once held back the ancestral kin of this flow.

Below the berm, dormant deciduous woods accompany the stream to the edge of dense, uneven-aged mixed forest. I continue on along the roaring watercourse into ever thickening balsam and spruce saplings below a sparse canopy. Breaking through the barrier with arms crossed in front of my face, blinking quick and slight, eye gouging evergreens give way to hip hugging hobblebush. From here the view opens.

There's a swamp with dozens of dead trees standing; ghost-grey remnants of evergreen life. A few blow downs add horizontal punctuation to the vertical vestiges while upended curly root disks throw a dash of chaos into the right angled order. Beyond the swamp, a hill covered in healthy evergreen woods provides contrasting backdrop to the tinder dry conifer corpses.

Back tracking, I walk upstream through the dried and drained beaver pond entering another area of thick, uneven-aged mixed woods. I've been lost a time or two in areas such as this by not paying close attention to where I've wandered into or from which direction I came. With the stream as my guide I continue some distance before reaching an old abandoned and layered beaver dam where the forest ends and a tussock laden swamp begins. Aside from an opening in the forest around the area of outflow, the dividing line between swamp and forest is sharp. Yellowing young spruce and fir nearest the edge of sodden soil foretell their early demise. I wander along the forested fringe and find a place to sit. The view out and across the swamp is good while concealment remains adequate. And it's quiet, away from the rush of cascading water escaping through faults in the dam.

As skies clear, chill abates. The first bird sounds of the day come from geese honking somewhere along the steady flow through the tussocks. Mallards quack in response. Tufted titmice sing their sharp Northern cardinal impression from shaded tree cover on the south hill while a Brown creeper repeats its ultra-fast, high-pitched declaration; "Hey-lookatthelittlebrowncreeper!" White-throated sparrows flit about exchanging shrill whistles calling, "pleasepleeeeeessombodysombodysombody," while Black-capped chickadees piercing whistle-turn-raspy, "shree-shree-dee-dee-dee," permeates the understory. After a flurry of activity and performances duly noted and appreciated, the singers vanish one by one into the woods, taking their melodies with them.

I linger, enjoying sun-cast incandescent rays through the trees. The shadow of a large bird passes in front of me. It's a Turkey vulture floating on dihedral wings; such grace and delicate balance for a creature with so malevolent a reputation. Delicate balance indeed. Why does this animal, designed by Nature, have such a reputation when its life is devoted to maintaining a delicate ecological balance?

I continue watching the vulture through binoculars. It scans the ground, in particular where I am, as it spirals aloft relaxed; in command of warm, rising air. It's a master of technique and the knowledge of thermals. While watching, I recall early excursions alone into the woods.

One of the first thoughts I remember having in those early wandering days was that Nature is neither malevolent nor benevolent, it is indifferent. It is often our perception *of* it, and reaction *to* it that determines our fate.

From that point on, I realized much of what was to happen in my wanderings, and indeed my life, was up to me; a frightening realization for a teenager. As it turns out, I would later discover, a group of fellows with such names as Kierkegaard, Camus, and Sartre already had like thoughts and arranged them all neatly into something called existential philosophy. Who knew?

Back to the vulture... the vulture... where is it? It was there. I was watching it. How could I miss it veering off its spiral course? I wait; nothing. In an unusual move, I break cover and walk to the forest edge to get a better view; still nothing.

. . .

Wandering back along the stream, then upslope, I head out of the forest pondering the dust covered thoughts evoked by the vulture and look for it often, to no avail.

"Free will determines our path, but the brain has a will of its own. With self-mastery comes skillful living."

In the Woods to My Left

Bright yellow sun heats from behind. Dark grey clouds lie ahead; fitting canvas for the ash white, dull brass and light grey of dormant birch and beech painted across it. Air and water compete for my full attention as I wander upriver into the wind.

Blue sky windows ease open as the Divine Sun pulls water vapor ever higher into the atmosphere. Cold dry air descends between warm moist clouds, stirring the forest below with gusts and swirls and spiraling updrafts, swaying trees and vacuuming leaves from the forest floor. Streams roar with joy while stepping down from the highlands to join their larger sibling.

Away from the river, a lone Myrtle; scout of the warblers this far north, sings its calming song of reassurance that spring has indeed begun in the dormant wood. They seem to know, these little birds, when the worst of the enduring wintry weather is over.

A Yellow-bellied sapsucker drums its staccato rhythm while a silent pair of Hermit thrush flits in and out of the spruce thicket. Quiet White-throated sparrows along a trickling rivulet scrape the soaked soil in search of something to eat. A woodcock breaks cover, darting through the understory with direct intent. I follow its flight with binoculars as it dissolves into the forest beyond an old Shagbark hickory in the distance.

Walking over for a closer look, I admire the tree's majesty; tall, straight, and armored with the most beautiful plates of stone grey bark; eighteen inches long and three to four inches wide, the tops and bottoms of which curve away from the tree revealing mocha brown beneath. Though not an uncommon species here, this one is uncommonly large.

Climbing a steep ravine to the flat saddle above, I enter an odd wood overpopulated with gnarly beech. It's a wind scoured place where the trees nearest the ravine are stunted; bent tops revealing the prevailing wind direction. Walking away from the ravine, trees are of normal proportions with little evidence of prevailing winds. It's a lovely, lonely place, yet I feel a commanding presence. I stop to eat and see what may come of the feeling. To my delight, a sense of being watched comes over me to the point which the hair on the back of my neck bristles. But this is not the first time.

My mind fills with memories and possibilities; bear, moose, catamount, Sasquatch? I chuckle as the list evaporates and reality returns.

Scanning the surrounding landscape with binoculars, I spy a hole underneath tree roots on the upslope ahead of me as far into the woods as my 10x50's can decipher. It appears as though the hole sees a fair amount of traffic in front of it. Being midday, I don't expect to see anything, yet I'm compelled to get comfortable and keep watch over my "discovery."

And then it appears...

In the woods to my left, a coyote stares at me as I turn my head without conscious forethought. It's beautiful. And close. There's an air of confidence in its body language, a gaze of wisdom in its eyes. I look around for more. It seems alone. Again I'm drawn by its gaze.

Back and forth the debate has raged over coyotes, coydogs, coywolves, and eastern wolves. Which are they? Which do we have here? Are they dangerous? I flip through the questions while staring with admiration at the individual before me. I've seen many coyote. This one is big, very big, the biggest I've seen in Vermont; tall at the shoulders, long legged, and reddish… a hybrid perhaps, but not a wolf… is it? It can't be.

Not wanting to be disrespectful, I cease eye contact, stare off to one side, and contemplate this moment and the wonder of this animal. Free will determines its path (as it does mine) while its brain fills with sensory input and reacts to the surroundings (also as does mine). But while it was able to detect me and approach me undetected, I was unable to define the sensory input or redirect the will of my brain (which conjured up images of various real and not-so-real creatures) beyond waiting to see what might be coming. I admit it's a poor survival strategy. Glancing back in the direction of the coyote, I'm not surprised to see that it's gone.

I search my words to convey what this unusual canid was able to without speaking…

Free will determines our path, but the brain has a will of its own. With self-mastery comes skillful living.

"Things we hold and nurture grow and evolve. But things we hold back become stagnant. Knowledge is for gathering up, adding to and letting go, not choking off and letting die."

Urged from My Pondering State

Chalk white smudge of translucent gibbous moon hangs low in the cerulean slate sky. Opaque blinding disk of sun stands high, opposite the moon... a welcome source of warmth on this cold spring morning. The trail ahead is clear of ice, yet muck awaits; product of sun warmed surface and still frozen subsoil. Seasonal streams run clear and crisp with meltwater from a nearby snow covered summit. It was a good winter there in terms of snowpack.

. . .

Further along, a woodcock springs up in front of me raising objection to my presence with percolating bubbles of whistle-chirp as it weaves through the loom of a nearby thicket. There's little wind. The woods are quiet except for streamers of birch bark strips that crinkle-flap and cast off limbless white trunks, crackling on every twig of understory as they fall to the ground; an inglorious end for such a beautiful and useful element.

The faint warbling song and chatting wren speak of a distant bird reaches my ear. It's too far away to confirm. I hold my breath and listen... Proximity sorts out rhythm and pitch and clarifies the phrasing as I smile at the first Ruby-crowned kinglet of the season. As is often the case with these and others of the smaller birds, it flutters ever closer, performing its peep-drawn dribbling melody directly above, a few meters or so feet from the ground, then continues on its way.

. . .

Clear songs of nearby titmice and Song sparrows and a single warning horn of goose in the distance greet me as I enter a labyrinth of swamps and ponds. The forest here is uneven-aged mixed wood and the perspective changes greatly from one swamp to another, with sun exposed flats and south facing hills to gentle north facing inclines covered in conifers, holding fast to their slow melting snow. False banks beckon the foolhardy as half-iced ponds linger in the shade, clinging to winter.

There are numerous beaver families in the neighborhood so I take time and care negotiating the labyrinth while pondering their industry; a matrix of mud, stick, and rock, assembled one piece at a time, creating a richer life not only for themselves, but to the enrichment and even the very existence of other's lives. What goodness comes from pure intent and its relevant action as we build our beaver dams of life and watch things flourish behind them. These dams must be cared for, yet no matter how much care is given, over time, they give way. This is natural.

Things we hold and nurture grow and evolve. But things we hold back become stagnant. Knowledge is for gathering up, adding to and letting go, not choking off and letting die.

I'm urged from my pondering state by a sense of being watched. A beaver floating motionless in the water nearby and another half in, half out of the water on the shore to my right, stare at me with a clear expectation that I should leave now that my thought is finished. Beavers aren't fond of visitors and even less so of one's overstaying their welcome. After a brief display of etiquette in the form of eye contact with each, I wander off in the hope of finding a wade-able way out of the labyrinth.

"Patience is more a product of cultivation than of any one thing learned."

Watching Ice Melt

As I wander out of the muck and ascend through deciduous forest, another woodcock pops from the ground and speeds off into the dormant wood. It's hard to imagine this evasive little cryptic-clad morsel being plucked from the air with primitive bow and arrow.

Cool west winds temper the exertion of climbing as I crest the hill above a large pond, ice yet within. This high elevation basin keeps a tight grip on winters' chill as there's no egress for the frigid air to escape.

Silence embraces me at water's edge as I nestle among low growing American yew and dense patches of wintergreen where the comfort of ethereal scent joins the cradling arms of silence.

Gazing across the frozen pond I notice a subtle transition as varying thickness of ice melts at different rates; progressing from dull white to ever darkening shades of grey until at last, a small dark spot of water appears upon the surface.

Patience is more a product of cultivation than of any one thing learned and if any one thing is learned today it's that watching ice melt is an exercise in cultivating patience.

Beyond the growing pockets of meltwater, a pair of male Common mergansers, accompanied by a female of the same, dives within a limited open area of pond; a familiar early spring sight. Indifferent to my presence they squirt out of the water one at a time onto the surrounding ice; flapping, drying, and preening their wings, till when satisfied at their efforts, they swing their heads back and sleep in the comfort of a warm spring sun.

"Waiting to see how things may unfold is good. Knowing when to move on is better."

Where Wood Frogs Gather

Today's Forecast: 100% chance of cornflakes underfoot as dry winds desiccate leaf litter.

Songs and sounds of woodpeckers, sapsuckers, titmice, chickadees, creepers, nuthatches, and kinglets liven the dormant wood as I wander through a recent, selectively logged swath of deciduous forest. It's open and airy with little damage to unculled trees; overall a good regenerating cut. There's evidence of deer and turkey, and clumps of bear hair on a grand old maple snag.

My pace quickens with anticipation upon finding an older skid trail tracking away from the newer cut. Who knows where it may lead? A lone Spring peeper's calming solo persuades me to slow down and mind my surroundings.

. . .

Sometime after, near a seep where Wood frogs gather to practice their refined choral performance, "Congregation of the Ducks," I accept their continued rehearsal as an invitation, find a nearby rock of some size perfectly positioned next to an away leaning tree, and make myself comfortable. With bright sun behind me and breeze from in front, sight, scent, and sound are in my favor. Warmth of sun feels good between shadows of tree, as air remains cool in the forest. Ravens play tag at the summit of a nearby mountain, their joyful expressions of raucous laughter tumbling down slope. The frogs carry on for a time until at once, silence... Could be a disturber is near. Pulling into an upright position I focus attention in their direction.

. . .

A branch breaks to the right of the seep. A Wood frog quacks in response... the silence of its fellows remind it to stay still.

. . .

More breaking branches, this time louder though no closer. Another Wood frog inquires who's there... another round of admonishing silence.

. . .

An explosive crack and multiple snaps resound with a clear indication that a disturber is indeed near, though now moving away. A single Anuran response echoes in the hollow... once again, another family-shun.

As ravens continue their boisterous, aerial game of tag at the summit, I continue my quiet, terrestrial game of waiting here in the wood...

. . .

After thirty or so minutes without obvious sounds of something traveling the forest or of Wood frogs' quacking chorus, I decide to leave. Waiting to see how things may unfold is good. Knowing when to move on is better.

The old skid trail led nowhere in particular, as is often the case, so I wander off in a direction that will take me out of the forest near where I entered. Two woodcock startle me as I approach, unaware, within a meter of them. I beg their pardon as they speed away in different directions expressing distain with asynchronous percolating whistle-chirp. Before moving on, I scan the surrounding forest floor for eggs laid in the open; not an uncommon woodcockan custom.

As I emerge from the woods, a White Admiral butterfly escorts me, its undulating motion a representative wave goodbye from the collective population of the forest. Or so it seems.

A Quieter Spring than Usual

The second mid-waxing moon of spring brings trillium plants with flower buds still closed tight, Trout lily leaves quilting the forest floor with few yellow flowers and the joyful green of burgeoning foliage resurrected from the sullen brown of dead leaf litter as False hellebore spring from wet places.

Blackberry leaves and the small leaf buds of White spirea begin to open while the buds of black and red raspberries remain closed.

Leaves in the buds of blueberry plants swell, yet wait to see what happens to other's leaves before venturing out.

Violet-turning-from-green Elderberry bud clusters stand resolute between fresh unfurled leaves.

Hobblebush umbel's outer ring of larger flowers; clear green-turning-white, advise the smaller, inner flowers, still clustered and tight.

Sapling beeches' lazy buds resist the lengthening light of day while older siblings' lively leaves unfurl from scaly sheathes.

Yellow birch lives a different life where sapling leaves emerge and leafless trees adorn themselves with dangling clustered catkins.

Maples of differing claims to fame show green in timely fashion while ash trees fashionably late tradition keeps them looking ashen.

On a nearby hill, crimson-orange aspread with red and yellow-green of untrue hue mock the colors of fall against the grey and brown of latent trees and last year's leaves. The colors here are richer and more varied than those of lower elevations now turning green, while the highest deciduous summits remain grey.

The wind carries few bird songs today... again. It's a quieter spring than usual.

"You can tell a lot about a person by the size of their fire."

Pinhole Points of Light

I wake to the muffled crack of a stick snapping into forest duff, my eyes scanning the quiescent woods illuminated by first quarter moon in this wee hour of the morning.

Echo beings that live near running water quiet their conversations as my focus hones with anticipation of footsteps. Shadow creatures busy themselves in silver white moonlight. There's a particularly large one, slow moving; unusual for shadow creatures. Another snap... a scuff of leaves and debris... This is no shadow creature.

I struggle with its outline against the nighttime woods as bright moonlight from behind it darkens my eyes, though its movements are familiar, its size unmistakable... A moose has ventured near. It appears nondescript in the pale of moonlit forest. As is their custom it stares a while, thinking whatever thoughts moose think, then wanders off in no great hurry; breaking branches and snapping sticks underfoot as it drifts away, while I stare at the sky and drift asleep.

. . .

My eyes open to a glittered veil of stars stretching across the dark dome of night; dainty, perforated tapestry, pinhole points of light. A tailed meteor, an Aquariid; descendant of Halley's Comet, disintegrates from its radiant; phosphorescent flash, smeared, now gone. I yield to the night's peace and return to sleep.

. . .

Orange, blue, and winks of yellow preserve my night vision as the eastern horizon waits for dawn. It's a modest fire, clean with little smoke. In the comfort of its warmth, with a pipeful of tobacco, as the forest draws her pre-dawn breath, I ponder my experience with fire.

Modest fires use less wood, require less work, cool quicker when done, still act as your friend in the dark without concerning the folks at the National Reconnaissance Office and best of all, need smaller burn areas that are easy to restore before leaving. I can't remember the last time I sat by the comfort of a modest fire without remembering a quote I heard many years ago...

"You can tell a lot about a person by the size of their fire."

It's a salty old saying from as salty a sayer, an astute observation of a seer as well. He was, "sizin' up a herd of us survival-course green horns, roundin' up and headin' out," for a month's journey through the deserts, forests, and mountains of southern Utah. Though the immediate reference was understood by all, a deeper intent seemed etched upon the face of this salty old cowboy.

I've spent a lot of time in front of fires since then and have come to understand (or perhaps interpret) the meaning and intent of that old quote: Fire is a litmus test of personality; in the same way that big ones make a lot of hot air... yep.

. . .

    The sky lightens as Venus rises, pulling dawn from under the earth. Through binoculars, the thick flexed bow of its crescent takes aim at the pursuing sun as a Great Horned owl heralds the growing light of day. A Wood thrush begins morning vespers, Barred owls yammer, coyotes yip and yap, woods robins join the chorus.

. . .

    Glowing coal-orange horizon cools to lavender then blushes pink. Blue wastes no time cleansing the sky, replacing all color before the yellow incandescent orb of sun casts warming waves of welcome light.

. . .

    After returning the area to its pre-fire condition, I grab my things and head for some home cooked vittles. Maybe I'll whip me up some sourdough biscuits, pork fat 'n beans, crackleberries, an' a pot a horse-shoe float.

"Take comfort in the neutrality of Nature and fear not."

Goblins and Doom

Most every spring there's a veiled period of seven to ten days that drags on without much in the way of visible progress in the yet-to-be-burgeoning woods. Though buds swell, birds arrive, ponds shake off the last of winter's chill and the ground begins to warm ever so slightly, the weather is most often cool, cloudy, and rainy, even snowy at higher elevations. This year it happened during the second waxing gibbous moon of spring through full moon and into the next waning gibbous of the season.

. . .

But today, spring is unveiling. As is her custom and as part of the neutrality, grandeur, and indifferent beauty of Nature, she unleashes a barbarian horde of hemoglobin gobbling goblins; great swirling clouds of black flies that follow Carbon dioxide emissions so that nothing that breathes escapes. To add a little irony to it all, the fact that we've made efforts to keep our rivers and streams clean exacerbates the situation as the little darlings need clean flowing water to reproduce successfully.

It would be negligent of me while writing about such bane to forget mosquitoes and deer flies and of course quite remiss indeed to leave out the multitudinous ground dwelling doom known as ticks.

My understanding is that they all hone in on CO_2, warm bodies, and are attracted to movement. So running away won't help and running through vegetation is sure to back fire.

Given that at least one of the aforementioned arrived during the Jurassic Period and all flourished during the following epochs of primate evolution (in which proto-prosimians appeared and produced a limb on the family tree that would later evolve into *Hominidae praesentem diem* despite the blood robbing occupation of omnipresent goblins and doom) I take comfort in the neutrality of Nature and fear not. I'm going wandering.

"It takes patience to understand beyond the hearing of a whisper."

Enduring Examples

    Strong west winds of dry blue sky
    sway old growth hemlock and pine.

    Ancient whisper of wind among them
    transcends place and time.

    In between there and here,
    then and now; I wander.

    Of what it is these elders speak,
    mere man can only wonder.

    My understanding is that ancient winds blew through something recognizable as a needle leaved conifer during the Triassic Period over 200 million years ago. That's a long whisper. Maybe we should listen... It takes patience to understand beyond the hearing of a whisper.

    So what would the trees say if they could speak to us? Or more importantly, what would we hear? On one hand, we see trees as commodities and this is right and just considering the usefulness of their wood. It's said you can't see the forest for the trees. But how far beyond their wood can we see? About as far as driving economic factors like future demand and projected price.

    For the record, I'm not a tree hugger. And I'm certainly not pointing fingers at anyone engaged in the business of cutting trees (a necessary, productive, and proud industry of good people earning an honest living) when I myself use them extensively. Simply stated, they're invaluable on the one hand. On the other hand, trees have something else to offer besides oxygen, aesthetics, and the aforementioned.

I've had the good fortune of crossing paths with some very large, very old trees. I'm moved to touch them, stand near them, look up through them and feel childlike wonder at their existence; what they've lived through, what they've endured, what the surrounding area was like when they were seedlings, saplings, and young trees, what or who has passed by or stayed for a while under cover from rain, snow or sun. How many droughts have they seen? How many fires came near or licked their trunks? How many bolts of lightning have they dodged or even withstood? How much water and how many tons of nutrients have they absorbed from the ground?

How many starry nights do these giant yet humble fractals reach for the Great Galactic Fractal in a similar way and with the same intent as I, when reaching for them; to feel the connection to something older and grander than myself? Yes, I touch these venerable trees because for a brief moment I connect with one of the most enduring examples of silent, stoic existence this side of life.

And maybe this is all they'd say if they could talk and we could understand… maybe… yes, I hear it in their whispers.

"The courage of conscience calls empathy to action."

An Interesting Game

Wandering the trails of moose and deer through a mixed-aged forest of balsam and spruce, I emerge into dense deciduous woods where all the young tender leaves are the same fresh bright green. Striped maple, Sugar maple, beech, paper birch, yellow birch, even bramble leaves have the same color in this brief moment in seasonologic time, as each has a different hue at maturity.

The woodland wildflowers have a different story. They're very much possessive of their individuality at all times of the year and have no interest in blending in. Trout lily leaves display their namesake mottling in a darker hue than the blending forest trees. Leafy green trillium evokes the memory of taste, as of something in salad; medium green and floppy-crisp. Columbine's more delicate design offers smaller leaves of a blue-green hue. Unfurling ferns; variations on the theme, are speckled with fine brown hairs.

An over abundance of ovenbirds strikes me; their mantra, "teacher-teacher-teacher-teacher," stays in my head as I venture beyond the dense wood and emerge into rolling, semi-open terrain.

A Chestnut-sided warbler's always polite, "please-please-pleased-to-meetchya," welcomes me, while the Black-throated green warbler's raspy, "zoot-zee zee wee-woo-zee," of pending decision, hangs in the growing humidity.

Common yellowthroat's, "win-Winchester-Winchester-Winchester-win," cheer for the southern England footballers, and the faint, "dwink-yor-teeee," of an Eastern towhee in the distance suggests Mi5's robotic avian surveillance program in a bird-brainwashing campaign.

In the sky above, ravens "gwonk" on their way toward a low hanging, late waning gibbous moon north of southwest while the faint chickadee-mocking-squabble-speak of Tufted titmice in the distance tickles my ear as I enter a quiet grove of mature Norway spruce.

The piercing two-note whistle of a Broad-winged hawk splits the air. I see its silhouette gliding above. It vanishes… there's another whistle and a gust of wind to camouflage the sound. I continue wandering through the spruce grove then travel along its edge, parallel with an old stone wall. There are apple trees in bloom on the other side; old trees, old as this wall. Together, they're a reminder of change, progress, regress, and the inevitable.

The hawk reappears, hop-gliding from tree to tree as I crawl over the stone wall into the old orchard. I stop to watch my companion through binoculars before continuing on. There are deer, bear, and moose tracks in here along with the scat of all three.

Wandering out of the orchard and continuing through open deciduous woods, I notice the Broad-winged hop-gliding around me in a counter clock-wise circle high in the canopy. I stop. It stops. I begin. It begins. It stops. I stop. It begins. I begin. It's an interesting game.

Curiosity getting the best of me, I find a place to sit and have a smoke. While preparing my trusty Savinelli Roma with a favorite tobacco blend, the Broad-winged calls, glides down to the lower level of the canopy and perches on a limb well within sight... a curious move. The sight of smoke coming from an odd shaped stick in my mouth doesn't seem to concern the hawk. If anything, it seems all the more curious as it glides even closer. This doesn't make sense to me and doesn't feel right. It's the winged equivalent of a bobcat walking over to see what I'm up to.

I play along, nodding my head upward in greeting. To my delight it does the same, twice. Now what? I've started a conversation in a language I'm unfamiliar with. I wait. It nods again. Not having the slightest idea what to say next, I puff on my pipe letting it smoke instead of letting the smoke out of my mouth. The hawk looks around with tilting head. I imagine it's reading the forest menu; mice, voles, a toad perhaps, maybe even a distant relative.

My understanding is that this hawk's primary prey is terrestrial. But I remember one summer at our house when robin song dominated the woodland conversation due to an explosion in the local population. That year, the resident family of Broad wings ate well all summer on a ready supply of red breasted fowl, young and old.

Though not my usual custom when this close to any of our woodland kin, I raise binoculars to look at the hawk. As it stares back through my objective lenses, I'm reminded of a lesson learned long ago.

. . .

As a kid, I was a sharpshooter at throwing stones. I threw stones farther and more accurately than most other kids my size and even took to wagering at the ripe old age of eight. One day while walking home from school with a few classmates, we spotted what looked like a hawk on the ground, wrestling with what looked like a rabbit. One of my comrades pointed toward the scrum as the hawk disengaged and took flight. Primeval instinct consumed me as I scanned the ground for a proper rock, picked it up, acquired my quarry and loosed my primitive projectile. Watching in virtual slow motion, it became evident that rock and bird were about to cross vector… Yes, I hit it. And downed it; to the accolades of my fellows. I was horrified.

Running faster than I ever imagined I could at that age, I arrived at the crash site before anyone else. The hawk was out cold, wings spread as in a museum display. It was the first time in my life when the courage of conscience called empathy to action. With no thought of consequence I picked it up as gingerly as possible and rushed home with it wrapped in my sweatshirt. When I got there, I cried.

After several nasty bites and a few talon punctures during the two days we spent together, the hawk waited and listened to my vow while perched on my gauntlet-covered arm, free to fly away. I promised never to do what I had done and with a remorseful tear, thanked it for living. As a last gesture it let me pet its cheek with my downward curled finger (all previous attempts ended in bites) before it jumped off my arm and flew away.

. . .

Lowering the binoculars, I puff my pipe again and raise my head in a nod. The hawk does the same and flies away. As I watch it weave through the forest, dissolving into distance, I recall the moment a few weeks after the incident when, while looking at an old picture book of birds, I was able to identify the one I had downed. It was a Broad-winged.

"A greater reality awaits on the lee side of the storms of life."

Indifferent Magnificence

One-hundred hours earlier, this area was covered with fresh snow. Now it's 85° F with gusty northwest wind as moist warm air rises with speed before a fast approaching cold front. I'm too far from where I started to get out of the forest before the storm arrives so I've found a suitable southeast facing slope near a pond, away from water's edge. Within the thicket of small spruce and fir I have a good view of the sky and reasonable protection from lightening, since the larger trees are on either side of the pond from me.

Darkness approaches as set sun and thick cloud create dramatic backdrop for the upcoming performance. There's excitement in the air. Wood frogs and Spring peepers, whipped into frenzy, dominate the woodland conversation, though Grey tree frogs cast a reasonable bid for "Heralds of the Storm."

. . .

The first rumblings begin, more felt than heard. Hermit thrushes, White-breasted nuthatches, and White-throated sparrows express their rising excitement in song. A woodcock flies off, too far away to hear its characteristic complaint. A beaver slaps its tail in objection to the upcoming interruption as it submerges and swims underwater to the entrance of its lodge, safe from the approaching calamity.

. . .

A deluge spills from the sky then stops. Frogs are still, birds have ceased. Cold quiet descends upon the hollow as dripping rainwater fills the gap of silence. I feel a sudden, sound dampening drop in air pressure and hold my breath...

My body jolts to an earth-bound Big Bang with a massive static discharge over the water. As my visual and aural senses recover, the storm arrives as do my doubts of staying where I am. Too late now, this is no time to move.

Another deluge spills from the sky; a great column of pouring rain and plummeting downdraft tens of thousands of feet long descends with a frightful roar. Sky flashes as myriad bolts of white light reach down from the clouds. In the stroboscopic sequence of swaying trees and windswept rain, the green of new leaves appears brighter than in full sun. Rolling crack-rumbles spread out in all directions. Windblown strata of rain drown the landscape. Violet and lavender hues flicker as cloud-refracted lightening colors the sky. Trees become negative photographic images for splits of seconds. Thunderclap echoes ricochet in self perpetuating sound waves in the amphitheater of surrounding mountains.

Surreal is a word that fades from meaning as I transcend reality into mild shock. Though unscathed by the spears, bolts, and whips of lightening, sensory input is overloading my brain. Overhead, all around, constant; light, sound, and rain assail me as my vision and hearing narrow. Panic pounds on the door of reason.

And then it happens...

I'm at absolute peace despite the will of my brain to save itself from the perceived threat by running away; an instinctive reaction from an entity that has no way of moving from danger other than to engage the body attached to it.

I tilt my head to feel the pelting rain on my face; open my mouth to taste it, smell the saturated air thick with the scent of sky and ground, see the bolts of lightning in every direction; clear white fissures upon a dim flashing canvas of violet, lavender, green and grey, listen to the cracking, whooshing, rumbling, splashing... It's a symphony of indifferent magnificence and I'm grateful for being here.

A greater reality awaits on the lee side of the storms of life.

"Many truths exist in Nature. Some dictate the occurrence of others though none negate the existence of another. There are no lies in nature."

A Moment of Privilege Afforded by Circumstance

Approaching a few steps at a time I stop… listen… wait… and begin again while following a spring fed rivulet toward a small pond, deep within the forest. A pair of Blue jays shrieks and swoops in the distance near water's edge. Hidden within thick cover of Balsam fir, Red and Black spruce saplings and deciduous understory, I examine the jay's area of interest for clues; a twitch of skin or ear, a moving twig or limb.

I see something but look away from the binoculars for a moment. Imagination can alter light waves entering objective lenses: A fact binocular companies don't mention in their literature. Focusing once again on the commotion confirms the ocular input. It's a bobcat. I see the back of its head with tell tale white spot within a wide border of black on each ear. "Chubby" right cheek ruff of fur and right front shoulder and leg are also visible through the dense, low lying understory. It appears almost an oversized domestic cat from this angle.

It seems odd for an animal who prefers twilight and nocturnal hunting to be wandering about at this time of day, though who am I to judge. "Seems odd" to me because I rarely see one. For all I know, this happens every day here. Besides, I imagine it seems odd that I've left the comfort of my home to wander among black flies and tickyweeds to get a glimpse of everyday life in the forested swamps, but here I am.

Living with three cats, I've seen a lot of different behaviors, not all typical for what we suppose cats do. But the bobcat in my binoculars is behaving very much like a typical house cat, and it's wonderful to witness this undetected. Kitten-like in movement, it bobs and ducks the swooping jays then all at once erects itself with a regal posture only to display kitten-rrific moves each time the birds approach. It looks more like play to me than a threat to the jays. But they're likely defending nest territory and seem to be taking this much more serious than the bobcat who, by the way, seems to have vanished.

Scanning the understory again for a twitch of skin or ear, a moving twig or limb, I don't have to search long.

A very non-kitten, regal looking bobcat sits facing me with a piercing gaze. Though honored by its undivided attention, I dare not twitch; staring through binoculars at one of our forest dwelling feline kin while they stare back is problematic at best.

Pink nose pad's flaring nostrils sniff soft breezes. Unblinking amber eyes; windows into its soul, peer into mine while watching for the slightest movement. Furred parabola ears locate and identify while tufted vertexes equalize sound waves for precise understanding. Broad furry cheek ruffs and long white whiskers compliment its wide-bridged nose. Dull fur coat of grey-brown fluff; silent to the ears and soft on the eyes, speckled with spots and lines of darkness, yields to a bright white breast. I watch it breathe as I note my own breath; shallow, silent. It's not fear of the cat that keeps me motionless, but the moment of privilege afforded by circumstance. I've watched it undetected and now it watches me, its fortitude unyielding.

Though my arms petition for rest, my thoughts wander, dissolving proprioceptor input from consciousness.

I imagine the cat crouching much the same way as my cats at home; wagging their hind ends prior to jumping at, pouncing on, or running away from whatever their imaginations have conjured up.

Wait…

Where'd it…

Wha…

Whoa…

Binoculars tug at my neck as the strap stops their fall. Without warning the bobcat bounds forward halving the distance between us then ricochets perpendicular to its original vector; me. Crashing through the forest with great speed and sound; a projectile unaffected by the laws of physics; neither obstacles nor gravity slow it down until it's gone from sight and sound.

I stand in awe and laugh at myself, the cat, the situation, and from the sheer joy of the experience. The bobcat never had any intention of attacking me. It was a clever and successful ruse to startle, rendering my locomotive powers useless for a moment which the cat used to run off; a simple strategy well executed.

Sitting on a rock I ponder the recent excitement. An inventory of truths fills my mind:

The bobcat was acting like a kitten.
It's not a kitten but a full grown obligate carnivore.
It seemed to play with the jays but would kill and eat them and/or their young.
It's an accomplished forest dweller with honed senses much greater than mine though it didn't detect me right away.
When it did detect me, it didn't sneak or run off but watched me as I watched *it*.
I didn't move.
It bluffed an attack.
I moved.
It ran away.
I didn't.
It could have inflicted harm.
It didn't.
I could have soiled my shorts.
I didn't.

The events of the encounter seem a result of the fact that many truths exist in Nature. Some dictate the occurrence of others though none negate the existence of another. There are no lies in nature.

An Embarrassing Moment

Refracting iridescent wings
flash violet-purple waves of light;
puffs of tiny forest fairies
on gentle breeze alight.

Cloud of bobbing dance display
moves sideways silent on their way;
a merry band that flit about
without the cares we care about.

Where they're from and where they go
few people surely care to know,
but I do wonder why they fly
and why their beauty caught my eye.

I've followed flight from left to right
and now my panoramic sight
reveals the reason I was led
to look around and up ahead.

The fairies turned my eyes to see
a big black bear that looks at me;
with quizzing gaze and sure mistrust,
it walks away in clear disgust.

"The Universe set in motion all things and all things are results of other things which may or may not be deserved or earned but happen nonetheless."

In Exchange for a Bit of Obliviousness

...And so passed the most embarrassing moment I've had in the forest since my unwitting demarcation of territory last year outside an occupied bobcat den.

Though I did ask in a gentle voice if the bear would mind coming back and staying a while, I was ignored. Non-threatening as it was, my peculiar behavior had a repelling effect on the bruin who had little interest in a hominid who needs a cloud of fairy flies to let it know it's being watched. What was it I wrote earlier? Ah, yes. With self mastery comes skillful living... a worthy goal I've yet to reach. On the other hand, to possess a bit of childlike wonder at my age is something I'll accept in exchange for a bit of obliviousness. Glad it wasn't a Grizzly.

. . .

The beauty and magic of floating violet-purple-puff-of-fairies notwithstanding, I should be more aware. This long forgotten and overgrown log road I'm on, though narrowed in width to a single trail, is a well used and crisscrossed area of the forest here. Bear, moose, deer, fox, coyote, raccoon, and fisher have all left evidence of their travels; tracks as well as scat abound.

Staying on the narrow, overgrown trail, I descend through thickets of spruce toward the ravine ahead where a boisterous torrent flows, draining numerous seeps and bogs from the gentle sloping highlands. With little difference in difficulty of travel between continuing on the trail and wandering upstream, I decide on the latter.

Groves of hobblebush filled with developing fruit; still green, yet characteristic in shape, line both sides of the watercourse below mature canopy, thick with this year's leaves. Pools in the stream reflect moss, understory, and the enclosure of leaves high above. Near the surface of clear water, an illusion of flowing algae appears. Everywhere, everything is green; exposed rocks, tree trunks, even my skin has a tinge of it.

Further upstream the ravine sharpens; tumultuous cascades replace boisterous torrent as the climb steepens. There are numerous toppled trees; strength of root unable to grasp near-vertical rock. Beams of yellow sunlight cast through clear blue windows heat the steep. Warm rising currents spin the air; winds swirl beneath the canopy. Less than one-hundred meters of elevation above where I turned upstream, it's a different world.

Pondering the beauty and magic of this little corner of forest I've stumbled upon, my mind wanders back to the incident with the bear. Though naturally wary of hominids, this black bear stayed and watched me gawk at a cloud of fairy flies it likely didn't see; *Ursus americanus* not being renowned for the keenest of eyesight. And I'm assuming it watched me approach and didn't arrive in the area after I did since despite my attention to the cloud of flies, the sound of a bear walking through the woods less than thirty meters away *would have* drawn my attention. I question things like this. Why did this bear, at that moment in time, allow me to approach as close as I did; curiosity or the behavior of a stalking carnivore? Why didn't it run or walk away while I was preoccupied, instead of waiting till I became aware if it? Was it curious, watching and learning? Maybe it too had a cloud of fairy flies occupying its attention. The forest is full of them today. My behavior was non-threatening so that rules out bluff charging, maybe. Today, this is what this bear did. Tomorrow, who can say?

    I consider it good fortune when visiting with our avian and mammalian kin and never take for granted their non-aggressive behavior, as unpredictability is part of their nature, same as ours. A good day today in the forest is no guarantee of not having a bad day tomorrow. Last year when I surprised a sow with small cubs she looked horrified at my proximity and took off through the woods in the direction of her young. Another incident with a big boar took two attempts at convincing him I was not a lesser being before he graciously gave way and wandered off. This year (thus far) another big boar wanders away, but in disgust; without conformance to the proper etiquette of eye to eye acknowledgement. Is my good fortune running thin?

    I'm not sure why, not being versed in neuroscience, but all this reminds of something I posed many years ago to a devout follower of a particular Belief who was insisting that misfortune comes to those who deserve it. I'd read a story concerning bears where a hibernating bruin's winter tree house was cut down at the commencement of logging operations. I asked the devout what they thought the bear did to deserve that, to which they retorted something to the effect that animals don't weigh heavily on the mind of the Omnipotent and I should not be concerned with what that Deity does with its creation.

If I remember correctly, the person's answer elicited an emotional response that may have even included an epithet or two. But if I had that conversation today, my reply would be simple and direct; a product derived from observations in the forest, including those of today: The Universe set in motion all things and all things are results of other things which may or may not be deserved or earned but happen nonetheless.

"Avoiding harm in the chaos that is the Universe is akin to being spared by the Unknown since the results of chaos cannot be predicted and are therefore, unknowable."

"Survival depends on strength of mind."

In the Dense Balsam Fir Thicket

With the last waxing gibbous moon before summer solstice came an end to a long cold spring... or did it?

. . .

36°F POURING RAIN FIERCE GUSTY WINDS ENE VISIBILITY NONE +4000' SOAKED HYPOTHERMIC EXHAUSTED NEED HOT BEVERAGE

. . .

Without taking time to explore my surroundings, I find shelter from the wind and rain within dense stunted balsams hugging the mountaintop. Memories of the last thunder storm and early season ice event blink by as I feel my strength draining.

. . .

The drenching continues, unhampered by tree cover. In seconds my small sheet of rip stop nylon is deployed, reflecting precious body heat, repelling chill rain. Another few seconds pass. I'm sitting on a pad, wringing hands over the warmth of a backpack stove heating water in a metal cup for Balsam needle tea; a belated attempt to thwart the onset of hypothermia while stuffed into my bivy sack, nibbling on carbohydrate rich snacks.

. . .

Sipping hot tea while listening to the wind and rain swish and snap my millimeters-thin nylon barrier, I feel a creeping morose resignation. I'm miserable; wet, cold. Shivers make packing a pipeful of tobacco difficult as I search the reasons for being here. Lighting the pipe brings no epiphany.

. . .

Shivers abate as warm waves of sleepiness wash over my rain-chilled body. A sense of peace permeates my being. Having finished my tea and put away the cooled pipe, I crawl deeper into my bivy sack for a nap.

. . .

A thunderous roar disturbs my sleep. Lumbering giants, dressed in loose, lightweight cloth swishing and snapping, appear through the forest all around me. Earth shakes as they pound the forest floor as if trying to squash a bug.

Crawling out of my bivy and leaving the shelter of nylon cloth despite the rain and wind, I confront them.

"You there," I call out to the one nearest me. "Why are you pounding the ground?"

"There he is!" it replies in a booming voice while squinting and sniffing, looking in my direction, but never at me.

Wait… I know these giants. They look familiar; not masculine but not feminine either, just giant, though their clothing is different...

"But that was a dream." I blurt out, louder than the whisper I intended.

"Your dream, not ours," replies the one nearest me. "You took our dreams long ago, befo…"

"Sshhh," hisses the giant behind the one speaking. "We swowr to brin' 'im bak wiffout sayin' nuffin'," it scolded in a grim, gravelly voice.

"We're looking for you," barks the one who spoke first, as anger grows on all their faces. "Did you think you would get away? You're back in our world now. And now you'll…"

. . .

The giants seized up and stopped speaking.

The rain dried up and stopped raining.

The wind blew up and stopped blowing.

. . .

"What is going on?" I call out with frustration into the cool, quiet air.

"You have been spared by the Unknown," a soft feminine voice speaks out of the forest, each syllable coming from a slightly different direction than the one before.

I know that voice, but...

"These giants pound the ground because they are trying to kill echo beings that live on and around the mountain."

"How do you kill echo beings?" I ask.

"More distressing than how is why," the voice replies.

"I know you," I say, shaking my head, "but for some reason I can't remember."

"I am Full Moon; sister of New Moon; one and the same; Bringer of the Light of Night, Stealer of Shadow. My spell on these giants will silence things in the forest so you can find and warn the echo beings. I know you're at peace with them. They speak well of you."

"Forgive me for disputing you," I reply with respect, "but I remember now. Didn't we establish that there is no Stealer of Shadow?"

In the most feminine of voices, each syllable now coming from a greater difference in direction than the one before, Full Moon replies:

"Stealer of Shadow is a name and a term and is true and correct. Without light there is no shadow. When I am my sister New Moon and there is no light, shadow, in a sense, has been stolen. But the shadow creatures that exist in your mind can never be stolen, they are yours to reconcile, yours to embrace."

I continue pressing...

"Something's not right here. If without light there is no shadow, then in no sense at all can shadow be stolen when there is no light. Your reasoning presupposes the existence of shadow whether or not there is light."

"You have learned well," replies the voice losing its feminine tone and lilt.

As my ears detect a rapid drop in air pressure and the hair on the back of my neck bristles, I jump out of the way a split second before a bolt of lightning strikes the ground where I was standing.

An ear splitting thunder clap wakes me... I think. I'm tangled and twisted in my bivy, rolled out beyond the cover of the nylon sheet.

"What's going on?" I whisper to myself, while crawling back underneath it.

"A test of fortitude," a low rumbling voice replies, moving away but still quite audible.

Startled, I look around in front of me then peek past the edges of my makeshift shelter. A chill travels up my spine. I see no one.

"Who are you?" I call out.

"I am Thunder."

"Of course you are," I reply with no small amount of sarcasm.

In an instant, brightness fills the landscape all around as a deafening crack shakes the ground. This is surreal.

"You have been spared by the Unknown," the voice says in a low rumble, moving away but still quite audible.

"I've heard this numerous times and it seems familiar," I exclaim with vexation, "but I can't remember... What is the Unknown?"

"It is your creation. You created the Unknown," the voice rumbles.

Concentrating is difficult. My mind keeps wandering from New Moon to Full moon and now to Thunder. I can't remember anything. Am I in a hypothermic hallucination?

. . .

A string of frayed memories blink by...

. . .

"You're right," I reply, remembering the early spring ice storm that brought down a branch, missing me by inches. "It was a thought," I continue, "gratitude, a moment of realization and reflection. I believe it was chaos that brought the branch down and chaos that it missed me. It seems a logical conclusion then that avoiding harm in the chaos that is the Universe is akin to being spared by the Unknown since the results of chaos cannot be predicted and are therefore unknowable. My proclamation that I was spared by the Unknown was an expression of gratitude, respect, and reverence for... well, the Unknown."

"Write about it, all of it," the familiar feminine voice speaks out of the forest, each syllable coming from a slightly different direction than the one before.

"Full Moon," I acknowledge the voice, with a feeling of warmth toward it, "what happened before? It was confusing. You contradicted what you, your sister New Moon told me earlier in spring and then your voice changed. There was lightning, and Thunder spoke, and…"

"You were falling into sleep," replies Full Moon. "Even now your hypothermia threatens you. Thunder and I worked together to keep your mind strong. Many things were allowed to happen to keep you from slipping; your mind was forced to think quickly, to look for answers, to adjust to changes. Survival depends on strength of mind."

"Please-please-hurry-hurry-hurry" begs a much higher pitched voice than Full Moon's. "It's time to go," it continues. "The giants are coming. They seek revenge for the past, befo…"

. . .

The sweet whistle of a White throated sparrow tickles my ears and opens my eyes. Sunlight carried on narrow beams through spaces in the dense balsam fir thicket warm my soaked clothing, sending chills throughout my body. Everything is wet though the air is crisp and dry. I sit up looking around, trying to piece together what's happening. Where's my rip stop, my pad, my bivy? Where's all my stuff?

My pack looks abandoned, full, sodden. Rummaging through it I find the rip stop sheet where it usually is... and the pad... the backpack stove... metal cup... Where's my waterproof notepad? Ah, here... Picking it up while kneeling on saturated ground; I read my last entry and realize what's happened...

36°F POURING RAIN FIERCE GUSTY WINDS ENE VISIBILITY NONE +4000' SOAKED HYPOTHERMIC EXHAUSTED NEED HOT BEVERAGE

I collapsed... It was dream... all of it.

"We're all part of the great circle of life and death. And from a circle there are many views."

A Diplomatic Approach

In the dimming dusk, bright sparks from a ferro rod blot out my vision as tiny flare of tinder sets kindling alight. Flickering flame begets shadow in the surrounding woods as I grow my fire with deliberate restraint, keeping flame and smoke to a minimum.

Above, Jupiter in the south and Vega in the northeast twinkle through breaks in the canopy as a full moon beams white from southeast.

It was a long walk in and I arrived later than I'd hoped but with enough time before dark to gather what I need for a few hours of fire. It's a nondescript place to be, but close to where I'm going tomorrow; a small undeveloped lake with a pair of nesting Loons.

There's a stream beyond the fire where echo beings yammer and play their unruly tunes. Sound bending heat waves warp, twist, muffle and amplify their efforts. An occasional pop of burning hardwood adds staccato accents to the unique composition; an orchestration of fire and water.

The local coyote clan introduces itself in a family howl. I get the feeling I'm unwelcome. They're loud and close with a wolf like quality to their chorus, not the familiar yip-yap yelping so common with them. Perhaps I'm too close to a den or chose prime hunting territory to spend the night.

As the forest quiets, my mind runs scenarios of consequence for trespassing their territory. I'll likely hear them trotting back and forth during the night. Perhaps a visit to determine how much of a threat I am has been decided. The night will tell.

Blue-green jets fueled by orange coals lift yellow lapping flames above a Striped maple log. Rising wisps of smoke whiten in beams of moonlight filtering through the trees while flame of fire casts a dancing glow upon the understory. Moths visit. Most avoid the peril of drawing too close. A few rush headlong in burning desire to find their way.

Barred owls call to each other from the forest. "Come and see," they say. "There's a hominid with fire." As is their custom, drawn by light in the night, they approach in silence and watch from a distance. They carry on hooting, echoes spilling into the silence of their pauses spreading and fading throughout the wood. A lone Grey tree frog inspired by owl hoot voices its approval of their presence as a Red fox barks from somewhere along the ridge to the east. The fanciful yammer of blaring caterwaul begins with a long duet of hooting… "uh uh uh uh-oww… uh uh uh uh-oww…" descends in tone as one inspires the other to full tremolo. As with coyotes, two can sound like many as the caterwauling continues with overlapping phrases, sudden stops and starts, calls and responses, and deep nasal whinnies that dissipate into the dark.

Silence returns.

A lone Spring peeper sings.

With a wail of the ancient voice of soul, Loons begin their nighttime tales from the nearby lake. Stories of a time when moose and beaver were giants compared to what they are now and when hominids lived without dominance over the land. I listen as wail, yodel, and echo meld into one sedative sound pulling me beneath the surface of sleep.

. . .

Thick, mature understory of mixed woods beneath massive pine trees six feet in diameter convey an ancient, undisturbed realm where something much larger than me tops the food chain. It's an unnerving feeling, yet the beauty of this forest is mesmerizing. Nothing I've had the good fortune of being in compares to this.

I'm at ease with familiar sounds. It's the unfamiliar ones that elevate my awareness; certain bird songs and calls, a frog possibly, and of course the heavy-footed scampering in particular draws my attention as I wander toward what appears to be an opening in the forest.

Sounds of running water beckon; not flowing, not rushing, more a collection of rivulets than stream or brook. As I approach, my brain has trouble accepting the ocular input.

This swamp is huge. There's an enormous wall to my right. It looks like a beaver dam but it's over thirty feet high. Numerous rivulets seep along its length which extends for a hundred meters or more... And the building material; this is no twig and branch construction. Small trees and large limbs placed and reinforced with mud and rock in signature style say beavers, but the size of the construction is too disproportionate to the size of the builders, at least the ones I'm familiar with... This is impossible.

Heavy-footed scampering draws close along the trail I arrived on. Pulse quickens as instinct takes over compelling me to scurry out of sight through thick vegetation along the water's edge.

. . .

Dappled moonlight through the canopy reveals at least one spying coyote as it trots by, my transition to reality from dream made quick by its presence. They've been busy while I was sleeping.

Focusing on night sounds, I hear them near; walking, scampering, sniffing. They're a little too bold so I rekindle the fire while maintaining its modesty.

I think about the coyotes while placing a striped maple stick into the flames. We're all part of the great circle of life and death. And from a circle there are many views. I don't know what their view is of me any more than they know what my view is of them. I've never had a problem with coyotes and even as close as they are tonight, I feel no ill intent. But they are free roaming entities who do what they want when they want and this is their territory. If they have exception to me being here, negotiating a peace in the form of a rekindled fire seems a diplomatic approach.

What Fish Think

Recent rains on saturated ground run rivulets of duff and silt through the evergreen forest. Partridgeberry and wintergreen carpet the memory foam padding of conifer needles at lake's edge where tiny deltas form as seeping sediments' endless land claim continues. I stop to examine a rock festooned with coyote scat and wonder about its placement. These markers are usually found along established trails.

The jaw-clenching, teeth-grinding whine and hum of mosquito hordes and orbiting deer flies threatens my sanity. It's one of those days when reality of roaming the woods in spring smacks the face of romanticism and culls the herd of hominids that holds that notion of the forest.

I follow beaver trails looking for a likely place to cast a lure. There are many likely places... likely to snag it in a tree or shallow. As my search broadens within shaded thickets of understory, a curious sound tickles my tympanic nerve; a single puppy bark from out on the lake. I stop to focus... and listen... It's the single note yip of a Loon.

Spotting a pair in the distance I watch through binoculars till my arms fatigue. I'd hoped for more than long range looks and a yip or two from the loons today after spending the night out nearby to visit them, but they've been quiet and aloof.

Lowering the binoculars, I notice sunlight dappled lake bottom nearby as a few fish drift over submerged boulders. Deploying my ultra-light gear despite the proximity of puckerbrush, I snap on a tiny lure and cast beyond them.

Roiling water surrounds the spinning trinket...

A tickle...

A tug...

A yank! Twelve inches of Large-mouth bass tries to eat and run. I reel it in, unhook, and return it to its fellows who seem all too eager for a go as they hover in the water, waiting for me to cast again. Even the individual of recent acquaintance rejoins the guild of the gilled that have yet to be grilled.

I oblige with another cast.

My wire-guided missile of retrieving doom soars toward splashdown...

T H E Y S C A T T E R.

So much for knowing what fish think.

19 Days of Merriment

As the last waning gibbous moon of spring moves toward third quarter, weather continues to do what weather does; change. One day ends in spring chill and winter fog, the next begins with clear sky that heats quick and ends dry only to begin the following day in spring chill and winter fog... This is the first June in memory where stoking the woodstove became a daily morning ritual.

Despite a changeable temperament, spring has a beloved constant; it begins the time of longest light. Summer solstice may get all the credit, but the difference of 1 minute in a day consisting of 1,440 of them doesn't seem worthy of all the hoopla; .000694 wouldn't draw much interest as an investment, why make such a fuss over it when it comes to time? This seems to contradict the adage, "Time is money."

But what if we consider a period of longest light rather than a particular day solely on the merit of 1 minute? Let's examine a period of time spanning a scant 5 minutes beyond the maximums of sunrise and sunset, in addition to their corresponding astronomical twilight times of dawn and dusk. It's important to include these times to get an accurate picture of the length of daylight within each day of the period. For reasons of accuracy a set location needs to be established, so the times and dates relate to where I live in Vermont.

There's a period of 19 days beginning June 11th and ending June 29th when all four events mentioned above are either at maximum or within 5 minutes of maximum. Using the first and last days of this period the times of the events are as follows:

June 11 2017: Time from crack of dawn to darkest dusk: 19:57

Astronomical Morning: 02:53
Sun Rise: 05:11
Sun Set: 20:31
Astronomical Evening: 22:50

June 29 2017: Time from crack of dawn to darkest dusk: 19:57

Astronomical Morning: 02:56
Sun Rise: 05:14
Sun Set: 20:53
Astronomical Evening: 22:53

As we can see from observing the times, June 11th and 29th are the same length in terms of discernible light. In between these dates the length of light is at its longest.

So I say, let's give longest light its due and stop qualifying one day out of 365 as the longest based on a .000694 difference between it and the ones before and after. Let's celebrate the solstice with 19 days of merriment and bask in the longest light.

"The unfortunate truth is that we often judge according to preconception instilled in us, not by exposure to something ourselves, but through an idea promulgated by others."

By What Standard?

A large doe and her whizzing band of wispy minstrels; a mosquito cloud, greets me as I enter the woods on this mild, humid morning. She wears a peculiar grin while allowing me a closer proximity than usual for a Whitetail. And a fawn is near. Her familiarity is puzzling.

Osmotic understanding seeps in while mother and young bound off and legions of needle beaks redirect their efforts. Having lost the deer's heat signature and trail of CO_2 emissions, they vector a new target; thin skinned and slow moving, emanating excess heat and spewing exhaust from the strenuous climb to get here. Fortunately for me, Permethrin and DEET make up for the aforementioned disadvantages, thwarting their repeated efforts to draw blood.

Though the most determined continue to pursue me as I begin the day's wanderings, my focus turns to the "feel" of the woods today; the "emotional" state of the forest. After weeks of rapid growth and deployment of biomass fueled by lengthening days and copious rain, momentum has slowed. There's an overall feeling of being settled. The sense of urgency is gone. There's calmness about the wood. Wandering through the tranquil forest engrossed in thoughts of arboreal inspiration, my focus wanes.

. . .

Stomping bipedal footsteps nudge me from inattentiveness as they scamper through nearby undergrowth, parting ferns and other herbaceous plants with a trilling meow rising in pitch and ending in raspy cat cry; a mother Ruffed grouse commences diversion. Log-drum echoes near and loud convey collusion from a Pileated woodpecker while another whinnies in laughter from a distance at my reaction to the aural disorder. In contrast, a Chestnut-sided warbler, pleased to meet me, repeats its greeting as I continue walking beyond the range of its voice.

. . .

Here the woods are quiet. Many of early spring's roaring rivulets are nothing more than trivial trickle-ettes despite recent plentiful rain. Birds are busy raising young; only pockets of song exist here and there as I wander, though it seems almost everywhere, vireos can be heard in the distance. As I continue walking, cool understory mist refracts heatless sunbeams puncturing the canopy. Their energy scatters. Air seems to phosphoresce throughout.

. . .

A second Whitetail appears as I emerge from cool-steam woods into sun warmed sauna. This one seems more curious and playful than the first, running from meadow to woods edge and back again with white flag showing and an impish grin. She's inviting me to follow; a clever diversion, a deliberate action. And I almost succumb. But her behavior says there's a fawn in the tall grasses of the meadow so I continue on as usual, circumnavigating within forested edge. There are several prints in the mud near a seep; some no bigger than my thumb's distal segment. Diligent mother as she is, she continues the wile till I'm out of sight.

Common yellow throats, Yellow warblers, and a Song sparrow invite me to linger as I return to deep woods while pondering the behavior of the mothers I've crossed paths with today. Two of the three employed ruses to draw my attention away from their young, the other, in her wisdom, used a different diversion. In all three cases I was allowed to approach closer than is customary for those animals when by themselves.

Let's face it. The concept of our woodland kin using creative problem solving to outmaneuver us isn't a topic of dinner table conversation, unless of course the discussion relates their failure to employ such capacity, while dining on one part or another of them. But there are numbers to support the idea that we are indeed being out-witted by our woodland kin.

Using the three most popular big game species in Vermont; Whitetail deer, Black bear, and Wild turkey (yes, turkey is considered big game) my understanding is that about 12%-13% of the estimated population of deer and bear along with 11%-15% of the estimated turkey population was harvested in 2016.*

* http://www.vtfishandwildlife.com

So by what standard do we judge the intelligence and creativity of these creatures? It's a question I've long pondered, an open question...

The unfortunate truth is that we often judge according to preconception instilled in us, not by exposure to something ourselves, but through an idea promulgated by others.

"While patience and understanding are good first choices there are moments when the ruse of having run out of them is better."

A Lot of Bluster

A lone titmouse sings a mourning song against the backdrop of quiescent woods as avian kin pause their daytime chorus. I feel its loss and pay my respects with a moment of silence and suspended travel before continuing on, up the mountain.

Jewel weed, a foot high, not yet in flower, grows in mire below the shading canopy of mature hardwoods. Violets bloom in less wet conditions with more light. Honeysuckles are in flower at woods edge near tall reeds growing in sunlight-soaked breaks in the wood. Sun cooks humidity to soup in open areas while the cool damp of forest favors mosquitoes. They're bad today… again.

. . .

There's sizable moose and bear track within the swamps and bogs at elevation. Stopping to examine a set of large moose tracks, I dent the soft ground with my own imprint, where, next to my foot, a baseball-sized rock lies at the bottom of a moose print three to four inches deep.

Blue jays shriek at a disturber in the distance. Something approaches…

I hurry toward the sound of water running and find a suitable rock to sit on with an upstream view; the direction of Blue jays warning. Though there's a bend in the watercourse about twenty meters away obstructing my view, I have a slight advantage sitting silent at streams edge with elevated banks on each side providing a funnel to draw my scent downstream.

A large form moves through thick cover of spruce, fir, Striped maple, and hobblebush. It's taller than I anticipated. A horse-sized cow moose emerges looking behind before turning her head to glance forward. Walking clear of thick cover, she looks back again, then forward, passing her binocular line of sight toward me without noticing. This isn't good. Her behavior says there's a calf nearby. I'm at a disadvantage to escape should she interpret my proximity and low position along the stream as stalking.

I no sooner think that thought than she snaps her head around and glares directly into my eyes. In a simultaneous exhibition of equal desperation we explode from our stationary positions... leaping grabbing hoofing stomping mudwaterduffrock pounding-hearts pumping-lungs flailing-limbs... It's a stunning display of primeval instinct. The only higher thought I have at this moment is the higher the better as I scramble up the stream bank toward small trees to employ as a barrier before I'm trampled. I push for the top with my life (perhaps literally) while she empties the small stream behind in a great splash where both back legs push on the gravely bottom in an effort to catch me before I reach safety.

From behind the relative security of the few small trees between us, I watch the moose slip and stomp the bank I was scurrying up a second ago. Her eyes are mad, her ears pinned back, her mane erect. She's snorting, wheezing, wagging her head. She charges up the bank again, this time threatening to come around the trees I'm using as a shield. Again she slips on the bank. Again she stomps and wags her head. I focus on small things in an effort to keep my wits; there's a slight breeze, jays shriek nearby, I've destroyed an ant hill with my shuffling. She charges another time with the same angle as before but the lack of momentum and soft bank work in my favor. Or is it something else?

There's a lot of bluster going on, but couldn't she clear this bank and whip around these trees if she wanted? The question begs to differ with my previous assessment of the situation. Maybe chasing me behind the trees was all that was necessary, the rest of this behavior being ceremonial in nature; obligatory bluster for the sake of maintaining dignity, and space between her calf and me.

I keep my composure while letting her know I understand she was startled by my presence and accept her behavior up to this point as defensive. I apologize, speaking in the best diplomatic tone I can muster, and assure her I meant and mean no harm.

The tense air around us takes a refreshing deep breath as she steps down off the bank and into the stream with all four legs. I glance at her calf, now browsing, relaxed. Knowing she's watching, I look at the cow again. The tension on her face is gone. It seems we have an understanding. I'm taken by how quickly the scene has changed. Did it change because I read her behavior and expressed understanding with interpretable inflection? Or is she satisfied this puny hominid is harmless?

She's quite pretty, least wise for a moose. Her coat is clean and rich brown without clumping or visible areas of tick infestation. I glance at her calf. It too has a clean, rich coat but much lighter in color. And it's cute. Flapping ears and twitching skin in response to deer flies, it's otherwise relaxed and at ease considering the stressful event that passed a short while ago.

My right leg stiffens with a message that it needs a break. I've had most of my weight on it since clearing the bank. Shifting weight to my left leg, a sudden sharp pain radiates from the back of my left foot. Seems in all the excitement I've strained my Achilles tendon.

As the moose overreacts to my shifting weight I remind myself to be tolerant of her behavior. Though she doesn't make an attempt for the bank, she does stomp in the stream and wag her head. I speak firmly while maintaining diplomatic tone and verbiage, reminding her that since we came to an understanding of the situation, she should tend to her calf and let me be.

Giving her time to think about what I said, I wait for an answer in the interest of maintaining good relations.

While I wait, the incidents of a few days ago come to mind when protective mothers took a different approach to my proximity. They used ploys and subterfuge to draw me away. This animal was much more direct. But then they detected me first, not the other way around.

Still waiting for confirmation of our implied understanding, I try to focus on sounds beyond the rush of the stream but all I can hear are deer flies' humming conversations concerning which of us is tastier.

Quite without sign or warning the young mother charges up the bank again. Convinced that she's rejected my assertion that we have an understanding, I force out a blood-boiling bellow and bluff a charge with raised arms from the safety of my tree-walled fortress.

The poor thing... I can see the terror in her eye as she swirls around away from me, clears the opposite bank, and lunges toward her calf with a much improved efficiency of movement compared to her blustering flailations toward me earlier. I dare say she exhibits grace and beauty in her escape. In a moment, cow and calf are out of sight, thrashing through the forest.

All that to say this:

While patience and understanding are good first choices there are moments when the ruse of having run out of them is better.

Getting Lost

I enter the woods with head down,
thinking thoughts unrelated,
preoccupied with things I came here to forget.
Sounds of memory echo within.
My mind's pictures are all I see.
How do I quiet my mind?
Why did I even come here?

I continue on; looking around,
gaining interest in this world.
Sights, smells, differ from where I live, sounds also.
I forgot what I was thinking.
I notice things I haven't seen before.
I should come here more often.

I sit on a rock and stare at the ground;
no thoughts, no walking.
Senses overrule my faculties. I'm anxious, cold.
Concentrating is difficult.
I shouldn't have come here.

"Examining clues before conclusion will help to avoid clueless confusion though clues without fusion or proof of collusion can still lead to theory, conjecture, illusion."

The Carcass

A shapeless enclosure of blurred greens and smeary yellows surround me in a midday chromatic mix, courtesy of sunlit glare throughout the understory. Within this world of fluttering color and shifting hue, yellow swallowtail butterflies glow green, floating about the forest atrium; leaves taking flight, each given a moment, returning quickly so the next can have their turn. It's a frantic scene, yet one of peace. Some plummet toward the green carpet below then rise again on leafy wings returning to where they began. Others flutter high above the forest floor enjoying the unfettered freedom of gliding till they too return where they began.

But a growing sense of the harshest reality of life seeps into this fantasy world by way of olfactory recognition. A whiff of something like mouse left too long in the trap oozes along the ground. I sniff out the sobering stench from upwind while moving with deliberate delay. I'm in no rush to get there but too curious not to go. Pungent pong thickens with each step till a swirling breeze erases the reek.

While waiting for the stench trail to return, my ears ring from the silence, my heart echoes within its chest. More than anticipation is at work here, more than curiosity. The hair on the back of my neck bristles. Maybe I should leave.

Wood frog tadpoles swim in a persistent vernal pool as dragonflies hover above. One or two hone in on vibrating wings of harassing deer flies whose humming seems disproportionate to their numbers.

The reek returns as abating breeze unveils the foul trail. Without the swish of shivering leaf the sound of humming wings grows clear. It's not the flies about my head but the hordes of them on something dead.

Instinctive faculties warn me against being here yet I walk toward the murmuring mass of ill bouquet where the forest duff is raked and piled; a mound of leaves and debris partially covering a carcass. There's hair all around; white hair, deer hair. The disturbed area is wide; over two meters, somewhat circular except for a pie-slice of untouched ground. The stench is retch inducing. There's red blood on clean bone showing, and deer hide.

But this is no infant fawn taken by an overzealous fisher cat. This is a full grown deer requiring considerable strength to down it. I embrace my sharpened senses; hearing, sight, and smell now affronted by nauseating wafts of rotting ruminant. Moving upwind for a moment while examining the scene, it reminds me of how my cats bury their doings in dirt. Coming closer, I look for clear paw prints or claw marks on the ground. Though motion causing the scuff was clearly one of raking, it's impossible to tell by whom or what.

Looking around for other clues, I walk in a slow deliberate circle, stopping every few steps to re-examine the scene from a different viewpoint while examining any disturbance on the ground. This isn't yielding any secrets.

Controlling my gag reflex, I move in for a closer examination of the carcass. The explosion of clear-winged scavengers as I approach pulls the odiferous air with it, scattering rank molecules that find their way through my nostrils and into my lungs. The thought gags me.

Moving duff and leaf debris with a large stick, I find the head somewhat intact. It's a doe. While examining it, the head slips off my supporting stick and flops over revealing the slimy black of stewed rot. Frenetic flies, seething maggots, rotting flesh and the stink of it all overwhelms me as I succumb to the eruptive force of repeated gag.

Staying upwind becomes a necessity so I walk a few meters in that direction and sit on a recent blow down. I wonder about the raked ground; an attempt to cover the carcass. Could it have been a cat? It would've had to have been a big one; a lynx or even catamount. Could it have been a pack of coyotes? Maybe they stalked her knowing her time was near. Maybe they happened on the doe while she was dying, or already dead. Or was it a bear or some other animal capitalizing on a similar find?

Why are there no vultures or ravens near?

And this sense, this heart-pounding, ear-ringing sense that transcends curiosity and anticipation; my instinctive faculties warning me to stay away. It's a vulnerable moment in which my mind busies itself stirring the caldron of conjure.

I shuffle my feet and feel something roll beneath them in the leaves. It's a spent cartridge; a 30-30. The cartridge is old; older than the carcass. Though rare, I do find the occasional spent shotgun, rifle, or handgun cartridge in the woods.

My line of reasoning gets a new tug. Could rare be the operative word? These cartridges are rare finds but they're here. Could this familiar carcass be the cache of a rare animal here in this area such as a big cat?

It's hard to say. But this isn't: Examining clues before conclusion will help to avoid clueless confusion though clues without fusion or proof of collusion can still lead to theory, conjecture, illusion.

"When a species such as sapiens is in their adolescence, they're so enamored with their own accomplishments that it's difficult for them to see past themselves and accept the fact that they're only a small part of the greater evolutionary equation no matter how much they impact things."

A Bird's Eye View

A Hermit thrush and ovenbird sing a lazy duet against the backdrop drone of deer fly swarms. Another Hermit sings a different dialect with curled finishing notes evaporating into humid air. Wandering toward the song in hope of recording it, I find a young tamarack in a sun-soaked seep; little cones of raspberry sherbet within blue-green clusters of stout needles against an understory background of lush green leaves. Though I search in ever-widening circles I don't see another. I wonder about seed dispersal; how did it get here? Was it anemochory, epizoochory, endozoochory or something more?

> What if the seed, in a windblown push,
> landed on fur near an animal's tush,
> causing an itch to which it did scratch,
> then cleaning the claw, to the tongue it attached?

> Then all the rest would be simple enough
> to place the said seed into foresty duff.
> So now we can see how methods-a-three
> Can all work together to make a new tree.

Pinched from my whimsy by the bite of a deer fly, I continue pondering... How far did this seed travel? How far did its ancestors travel and by what means, to get where *they* were? Where did they begin?

Sometime during my searching, whimsy, and querying, the Hermit song I'd hoped to record stopped.

It's a sleepy day with heavy air, one that urges me to nap within dry shade away from the seep. After quick deployment of my tiny screen tent, I crawl in, escaping the constant harassment of deer flies.

Listening to Red-eyed vireos chant their questioning mantras, I wonder about the collective wisdom of birds concerning *H. sapiens*. No other animals see us so readily, so collectively, and from the vantage point of time immemorial.

Sitting in the forest? They see you. Sneaking off to go pee or commit endozoochory? They're there. Having a snack, sipping a spring? There too. Skinny dipping a cool stream? Yep, their peering eyes are watching.

We're so used to them being everywhere, we don't notice them anywhere. Ask the average busy person how many birds they've seen today. See what they say.

And the birds know this. How many other free living animals stay within sight of us, often close sight? Because of their unique ability to escape, they, for the most part, are unbothered by our presence, adjusting when necessary to a more acceptable vantage point at which to spy on us; free to watch from whatever distance they feel comfortable.

I recall an incident many years ago while planting a bed of waxed begonias when a curious Ruby-throated hummingbird, apparently unable to resist the vivid red flowers, changed my conception of bird behavior forever.

In a stationary genuflection with trowel in hand, I kept still as it sampled each of the dozens of recent plantings no matter how close to me they were. In a magnificent display of aerial excellence this Lilliput aviator hovered from bloom to bloom fanning my limbs with feathery breezes. On an air cushion of its own making, within millimeters of my arms, legs, and bottom, maneuvering with confidence above and below, around and between; it performed lateral, vertical, forward, and reverse movements with equal ease until tiring of the activity and speeding off into the nearby woods. I've never understood the risk it took other than having since come to the conclusion that hummingbirds tend toward the foolish side of confidence in their ability to escape danger. They're excellent at it, and they know it.

. . .

I close my eyes and begin to drift off, listening to what appears to be a growing ensemble of bird song as I revisit the thought of birds having a veritable encyclopedic understanding of the ways of *H. sapiens*.

. . .

"I told you he was going to sleep," sings the Hermit thrush, with composed certainty.

"Yes, I knew it too," sings the other, with equal assurance and a slight curl in its fluty, ending notes.

"I don't TRrust them TRust them TRust them TRust them" fusses Ovenbird. "I watCH them watCH them watCH

watCH them from the ground and if you ask me, they're always sneaking around."

"I don't mind them," a whistle-warbling voice comes from the distance and arrives near. "Sometimes they're nasty, sometimes they're not. But you never know. Do you?" continues a Red-eyed vireo in its typical questioning way of speaking. "They don't bother me. Do they? No, though I like to keep my distance. Don't I? Yes, and prefer to stay hidden. Don't you? When they're near I mean. No?"

As a Black-throated green warbler flits within sight I hear it mumble something about seeing...

"I see something, see?" it says. "See, see, I see something. You see what I see? I see something in them that scares me. Their hearts are confused. They're not trustworthy. See, see, see, you see?"

"I know they can't always be trusted," replies the first Hermit," but like us, they're all different. We can't judge them by our experience with one or even a few."

A great tumult arises in the forest as robins and grosbeaks, tanagers, and a Wood thrush arrive and begin speaking, or is that singing, all at once.

"One at a time, please." insists the second Hermit, in a polite and diplomatic tone.

"I agree with Hermit," sings the Scarlet tanager in rich, buzz-bubble notes. "They usually don't see me, but when they do, they stand there gawking as though I were some rare species they just discovered," Scarlet says with a chuckle. "Sometimes it's cute, other times it's creepy, but none of them has ever done anything to threaten me."

"I feel the same as Scarlet," sings the Rose-breasted grosbeak in perky clear notes, rising and sinking as they bounce along. "I get fewer gawking stares but none of them has ever threatened me either."

"Thank you, Rose," says Scarlet.

"You're welcome Scarlet," says Rose.

"You're welcome Scarlet thank you Scarlet," mocks Robin. "You're mistaken! These are bad people!" he peeps. "There are way too many of them and they're ruining everything. You both move away during the winter but I stay close by. These people can't take the cold. They burn trees! And who knows what else to stay warm… Come on… they live in boxes… or caves… or whatever those things are that they build… ugly dwellings, nothing like our beautiful nests."

The fluty warbles of a Wood thrush percolate through the canopy as it too complains about us.

"Everywhere you go these days, these… what did you call them?"

"People," peeps Robin.

"Yes, people," continues Wood thrush, "they've been doing a lot of building of those boxcave things…"

"Ugly dwellings, nothing like our beautiful nests," repeats Robin, with disgust.

"Yes, well," continues Wood Thrush again, "my closest relatives and I are having trouble finding places to live. I miss seeing our cousins Swainson and Bicknel. And even our good relation Veery is having trouble. Honestly, I don't know how you do it cousins," exclaims the Wood thrush, now looking at the two Hermits, "but you seem to be doing ok."

"We arrive early," both reply, calm as always.

"Yes, the early bird gets the worm," sneers Robin. "Rubbish."

Whooping wing beats approach as Raven begins speaking before landing on a branch above me. Resisting the urge to look, I keep my eyes closed and continue listening.

"They're adolescent, I'll give you that," croaks Raven. "But we've had a relationship with them since before they could stand on two legs like we do. They can be dangerous, yes. But they're smart too, almost clever by our standards, and you have to understand that when a species such as sapiens is in their adolescence, they're so enamored with their own accomplishments that it's difficult for them to see past themselves and accept the fact that they're only a small part of the greater evolutionary equation no matter how much they impact things. Adolescent species never embrace the reality that time is the great equalizer. And Hominids have always had the most difficult time accepting this."

"Yes," interrupts Robin with bitterness in his peeping, "Because they think too highly of themselves. For *instance, some of them came here from another place and now look… spread all over the land from one side to the other and…"*

"Enough!" Gwonks Raven, in a direct and chiding tone. "So have robins. They're everywhere also. Does that make you all bad?"

Robin hops down from his limb and begins foraging for worms in silence as Raven continues speaking.

"Think of how long it took all of us to evolve from our earliest ancestors and how many of them have disappeared. It's different with sapiens in that they're the only hominids left. They have no other options. They have no close relations."

"They have no close relations because they kill each other off," replies the sad voice of Vulture, circling above. "We know because we've cleaned up after their fights too many times to mention. They don't even taste good, but that's our duty. We do it because that's what we do. It doesn't make us bad, but they treat us that way."

Robin peeps in laughter and flies away.

"I know." says Raven, in a somber tone. "They are who they are. But we are who we are, and ravens will honor our long relationship with them to whatever end."

A hush descends upon the wood…

. . .

I sit up in the tent and look around. It's quiet, silent even. Only when I slip out of the screen shelter do I notice trees filled with birds of many species and a raven no more than ten feet away and ten feet above. It's perched looking at me with a sideways glance quite common among ravens. Out of respect for this old soul I wait, allowing it time to decide what to do next. With a pre-note knock as though clearing its throat, the bird issues soft phrases common for an adult with young, while its body language stays relaxed and inviting, emphasizing the importance of what's being said. After a few moments of what sounds to me like repeated phrases, it stops moving and grows silent again. A sense of déjà vu washes over me.

"Yes," I say in a soft tone, "that day on the mountain. It was you. I've been thinking about what you showed me that day, how the Universe has many voices, all worthy of speaking, all worthy of listening, and all able to be understood... But everything that was said here... is it true? Are we known to be untrustworthy, destructive? Do birds really look down on us, well, of course you do, but I mean look down your beaks at us? And what you said about us being adolescent... Is it the condition of sapiens that we slog through this adolescence as the ages pass before we mature as a species? Is it that simple yet profound, precarious and unavoidable?

Jurassic inspired Oligocene yowls of *"Y-E-S-Y-E-S-Y-E-S-Y-E-S"* split the air as Raven answers my inquiries.

. . .

    Bellowing raven croaks jolt me from sleep; eyes wide open, breath suspended, motionless in my tent as reality orients. The Old Soul rocks back and forth on a limb above me and bursts into flight on whooping wings and witchy screams.

    I exhale as it slips out of the canopy.

"Silence is the balance of all things; stoic in the face of tempest, self-possessed in times of trial. It is the end of wisdom, the step beyond reason; the humility of understanding."

In The Beauty of Growing Darkness

In the last days of spring, as waning crescent moon diminishes toward new moon, soaking rains and waves of thunderstorms satiate a thirsty, reborn forest; filling her lakes and rivers, ponds and streams. Between nighttime thunder-beckoned downpours, lightening bugs reach their peak, honoring their name.

. . .

Arriving at sunset on the last full day of spring with plenty of time to gather wood for a fire, I notice clouds moving from the southwest against a darkening eastern sky. Billowing pillows of grey and white and shaded striations of blue mimic an early autumn skyscape. The air has a welcome crisp, though the forecast warns of a return to soup as seasons change hands, hours from now. But at *this* moment, in a clearing high above the valley below, I enjoy the respite from humidity, fog, and rain.

Serpentine sound waves lilt through the clearing as a veery spins its spiral song; farewell bid to Vernal Divine, pledge to summon summer sun, before the light of morn.

Though southwest winds blow clouds away, the air around me hangs. Hordes of mosquitoes assemble at the gate of DEET, threatening to breach my resolve. I fill my tobacco pipe and light it, bracing the gate, strengthening my wall of will.

. . .

With my tiny screen tent prepared for the night and enough wood gathered for an hour or two of fire, I settle in for the evening and ponder a season's passing: The blizzard a week before spring began, the ice storm early on, cool wet conditions throughout, yielding only its temperatures to the recent warm wet of seasons' end. Weather has been the main event; a soaker compared to the spring of 2016. I chuckle as my favorite, and sometimes annoying (or so I'm told) weather quote comes to mind. "Weather is what weather does."

And with what it does it commands the timing of what happens below it. Spring was "late" in coming this year. Migrating bird arrivals were postponed affecting distribution, nesting claims, and hatching schedules. Flower blooming was halted changing pollination timetables. Late leafing tree species leafed out later than late. Fish, I've heard, didn't take the bait. Spring peeper season came later than in recent memory and early season woodcock displays were grounded. From what I've seen, our larger mammalian kin birthed on the latter end of their seasons while the explosion of vegetative growth this year yields a forest as lush as any I can remember. Though all the beaver dams I'm familiar with have withstood the rains, I did hear of one I haven't been to that burst under the increased load.

And then there's the work and play that's halted and/or effected; logging, farming, infrastructure projects, building, gardening, painting the house, mowing the lawn...

hiking, boating, fishing, biking, swimming, camping, ball games, even napping on the hammock.

As if on cue the cloud above me wrings out its vaporous filaments with a brief downpour. Looking up at the now damp sponge of cloud moving northeast, I thank it for its gift and wonder if clouds understand sarcasm.

. . .

Gazing at the dimmed afterglow of sun through clear sky defiant of forecast, my thoughts focus on whether or not to honor the pagan sacred by welcoming the change of season with firelight. Though ancestral spirits implore me, I consider my location in the beauty of growing darkness, illuminated only by the shimmering green phosphorescence of innumerable lightening bugs. Absolute black of woods' edge glows in their collective light. Surrounding meadow glistens with their bioluminescence. Heaven above and earth below sparkle with their twinkling asynchronies. Illusions of green-tailed meteors smudge the jeweled sky... I decide against a fire.

My ancestors grumble as distant thunder conveys their disapproval. Raising my head with a tilt westward, I smile and nod, vowing a compromise in respect.

. . .

One minute before the arrival of summer solstice, I spark my tinder bundle, allowing it to burn as spring turns to summer; thus appeasing the spirits of my ancestors. Nothing stirs, not even wisps of web clinging to spindly stems. Here in the great deafening silence of the wee-est hour in the darkest night, among the holy bioluminescence of thousands of gatherers, as flickering flame honors the pagan sacred, here; at twenty-four minutes past midnight, summer arrives... as does an owl in silent alight on leafless limb, no doubt drawn by flickering flame.

It's a Barred owl, same as the last night of winter passed. Though I'm a long way from where I was that night in many senses, its presence lends to the feeling that a circle is closing, a journey's completed.

Through the eye of binoculars, tiny floating phosphor green lamps blink and twinkle, illuminating the body of the Barred owl as they orbit its form against the background of an unending, ever-expanding universe. It stares at me and blinks. My thoughts wander to the first moment of spring when another owl inspired me to wonder at the most abundant element in the Universe; silence; the ordered condition within the construct of chaos.

Silence is the balance of all things; stoic in the face of tempest, self-possessed in times of trial. It is the end of wisdom, the step beyond reason; the humility of understanding.

The owl blinks again. Turning its gaze toward Polaris, it flies north in silence, disappearing into the night.

Wisdom of the Vernal Woods

- Silence is the balance of all things; stoic in the face of tempest, self-possessed in times of trial. It is the beginning of wisdom, the step before reason; the willingness to learn.

- The simple emotion of gratitude transcends our conscious thought and gives humility to reason. Gratitude is the most elemental form of worship. It needs no adulterating, it has no equal. Gratitude is the purest act of genuflection.

- The Universe has many voices. All are worthy of speaking, all worthy of listening, and all may be understood... but not by all.

- The Universe began with a great light, and with light comes shadow.

- Things are not always what they seem.

- Shadow is a reflection of fear, and a way for us to reconcile those fears.

- Speech has the power to chide or instruct, injure or heal, raze or restore hope. It is our best tool and worst weapon, finest trumpet of all things good, warning horn of a darkened heart. All good and bad begin and end with a timely spoken word of men.

- Nature is neither malevolent nor benevolent, it is indifferent. It is often our perception *of* it, and reaction *to* it that determines our fate.

- Free will determines our path, but the brain has a will of its own. With self-mastery comes skillful living.

- Things we hold and nurture grow and evolve. But things we hold back become stagnant. Knowledge is for gathering up, adding to and letting go, not choking off and letting die.

- Patience is more a product of cultivation than of any one thing learned.

- Waiting to see how things may unfold is good. Knowing when to move on is better.

- You can tell a lot about a person by the size of their fire.

- Take comfort in the neutrality of Nature and fear not.

- It takes patience to understand beyond the hearing of a whisper.

- The courage of conscience calls empathy to action.

- A greater reality awaits on the lee side of the storms of life.

- Many truths exist in Nature. Some dictate the occurrence of others though none negate the existence of another. There are no lies in nature.

- The Universe set in motion all things and all things are results of other things which may or may not be deserved or earned but happen nonetheless.

- Avoiding harm in the chaos that is the Universe is akin to being spared by the Unknown since the results of chaos cannot be predicted and are therefore, unknowable.

- Survival depends on strength of mind.

- We're all part of the great circle of life and death. And from a circle there are many views.

- The unfortunate truth is that we often judge according to preconception instilled in us, not by exposure to something ourselves, but through an idea promulgated by others.

- While patience and understanding are good first choices there are moments when the ruse of having run out of them is better.

- Examining clues before conclusion will help to avoid clueless confusion though clues without fusion or proof of collusion can still lead to theory, conjecture, illusion.

- When a species such as sapiens is in their adolescence, they're so enamored with their own accomplishments that it's difficult for them to see past themselves and accept the fact that they're only a small part of the greater evolutionary equation no matter how much they impact things.

- Silence is the balance of all things; stoic in the face of tempest, self-possessed in times of trial. It is the end of wisdom, the step beyond reason; the humility of understanding.

About the Author

A Vermont resident for thirty-four years, J. E. Diaz has wandered woods east and west as well as abroad. A keen observer of the natural world, his first book, *Wandering Spring, Notes from the Woods of Winhall, Vermont* is an intimate journey of short stories that introduce his unique perspective. The overwhelming positive response to that first book prompted the creation of *Wisdom of the Vernal Woods*, with future plans to continue weaving non-fiction and fiction against the backdrop of Nature.

J. E. Diaz lives in Vermont's Green Mountain National Forest.

As always, your comments are welcome.

jediaz.com

jed@jediaz.com

www.ingramcontent.com/pod-product-compliance
Lightning Source LLC
Chambersburg PA
CBHW060526080526
44586CB00012B/638